ALSO FROM

CHRISTIAN

By J STAFFORD WRIGHT

Christians
and the
Supernatural

J STAFFORD WRIGHT
A key to understanding mysterious events

There is an increasing interest and fascination in the paranormal today. To counteract this, it is important for Christians to have a good understanding of how God sometimes acts in mysterious ways, and be able to recognize how he can use our untapped gifts and abilities in his service. We also need to understand how the enemy can tempt us to misuse these gifts and abilities, just as Jesus was tempted in the wilderness.

In this single volume of his two previously published books on the occult and the supernatural (*Understanding the Supernatural* and *Our Mysterious God*) J Stafford Wright examines some of the mysterious events we find in the Bible and in our own lives. Far from dismissing the recorded biblical miracles as folk tales, he is convinced that they happened in the way described, and explains why we can accept them as credible.

The writer says: *When God the Holy Spirit dwells within the human spirit, he uses the mental and physical abilities which make up a total human being . . . The whole purpose of this book is to show that the Bible does make sense.*

And this warning: *The Bible, claiming to speak as the revelation of God, and knowing man's weakness for substitute religious experiences, bans those avenues into the occult that at the very least are blind alleys that obscure the way to God, and at worst are roads to destruction.*

ISBN 13: 9-780-9525-9564-9
222 pages 5.25 x 8 inches £8.95 and US $12.95
Available from bookstores and major internet sellers

To the many students
whom I have taught,
and with whom I have learnt much

THE SIMPLICITY
OF THE
INCARNATION

J STAFFORD WRIGHT

Original writing ©1985 J Stafford Wright
This publication ©2011 C Stafford Wright

ISBN 978-0-9525-9563-2

PUBLISHED BY
WHITE TREE PUBLISHING
28 FALLODON WAY
BRISTOL BS9 4HX
UNITED KINGDOM

CONTENTS

PUBLISHER'S NOTE

This book is from a completed manuscript found in the papers of J Stafford Wright following his death in 1985. It was the final draft, complete with dedication, although for reasons that are now unclear it was overlooked for publication and is published here for the first time. It is a concise and well reasoned case for accepting the Biblical version of the incarnation of our Lord and Saviour, Jesus Christ, the Son of God.

In 1985, the number of English translations of the Bible was limited. J Stafford Wright, a renowned evangelical Bible scholar and expert on Biblical Hebrew and Greek, carefully selected each Bible quotation from the versions that were then to hand. This was not to back up theories or ideas that were out of line with other translations, but because in the writer's view the versions quoted here most accurately portray the meaning of the original Greek language in each instance. In most cases, our more recent English translations have very similar wording.

The book that follows is from what is clearly the author's final draft that had been typed by an outside agency, but shows no signs of being subsequently checked or revised by the author. Only typos have been fixed in this book.

FOREWORD
By J I Packer

When Canon John Stafford Wright, beloved former principal of Tyndale Hall, Bristol, died in 1985, he left this book complete; only now, however, more than a quarter of a century later, does it see the light of day. It is my privilege to welcome it into the world at last, and to call attention to some of its virtues. As I do so, I find myself thinking that Bible-believers have been the poorer for its non-appearance over these years.

In academic circles this little volume would be called a Christology, which means a study of the person, place and mediation of our Lord Jesus Christ, past, present and future, within the Trinitarian frame in which the New Testament sets it. This, of course, is the central core of real Christian faith.

While written at the level of the thoughtful but non-technical Bible student, the entire substance of the book belongs to the world of mainstream Christian orthodoxy, and the many imaginative touches that bring the material down to earth will evoke for many readers deeper insight into the basics than they had before. (And one particular argument, showing why the incarnation requires a miraculous virgin birth such as the New

Testament affirms, seems to me quite momentous in its force.)

The title, *The Simplicity of the Incarnation*, might seem to weigh the book down, for 'simplicity' in a positive sense is not a very common usage these days. What the author means by it, however, is exceedingly positive: reasonableness, straightforwardness, logical clarity and coherence, and, in a word, good sense – qualities in which the book excels, as did he.

Stafford Wright's special genius as a teacher was that he could sort out just about any area of confusion in any field of study and set it forth with a luminous clarity for which 'simplicity' was truly the fitting label. That is the quality that shines out here, along with the honesty, humility and good judgment that are the constant hallmarks of mature scholarship.

One does not have to agree with every opinion expressed to recognise in Wright's easy-flowing English the breadth of learning and wisdom, and the high standard of thought, that have gone into the making of this book.

So I welcome Stafford Wright's final literary legacy, and I say to all who love the Lord Jesus: enjoy.

Canon Dr J I Packer
Vancouver
Canada

PREFACE

Christians today are constantly told that they must rethink their beliefs. It is always necessary to do this, but now the implication is that they must modify, or change some of the fundamentals that are summarised in the historic creeds. This book is a rethinking of the Christian faith, but with the conclusion that modern knowledge can strengthen rather than minimise the truths that have been held by the Christian church down the ages.

I have based my book on the Bible, since it was the Bible from which the statements in the creeds were drawn. There is no fresh evidence outside of the Bible, unless one counts the Turin Shroud, on which any theologians can draw for assessing the great doctrines of the virgin birth, the resurrection and other truths. So I invite the reader also to start with what the Bible says, and then ask whether this still makes sense today.

The title of the book may sound strange, but it suggests that if one takes the New Testament seriously, as the early Christians did, a simple plan emerges, centred on our Lord Jesus Christ. I say to you, in the words of William Blake:

I give you the end of a golden string,
   Only wind it into a ball;
It will lead you in at Jerusalem's gate,
   Built in Jerusalem's wall.

After I had completed the book I came across some words by the late Harley Street doctor, AT Schofield, whose writings have been of great help to me, although few know them now. In his book *The Goal of the Race*, he writes: "In this discussion I shall draw my arguments from the original sources of the Faith ... seeking to go direct to the fountain-head, rather than to the somewhat muddy and troubled stream of current dogma."

He continues, "I shall try to present my theme in the simplest and clearest words that a subject so profound permits; and feel sure that I may look to my readers for a patient and sympathetic consideration of the arguments I shall advance."

That is what I also have tried to do.

Although this is not a devotional book, I have found that the excitement of true doctrine is a powerful incentive to devotion.

J Stafford Wright
Bristol

INTRODUCTION

If the incarnation, God becoming Man, is a fact, clearly this cannot by any manner of means be called "simple". Yet hundreds of thousands of Christians have found their satisfaction in so-called simple faith, as follows:

Jesus Christ was not only a good Man, but he was, and is, God, who at a definite period of time became truly Man through being born of the Virgin Mary. He lived a perfect life, died for the sins of the world, and rose again from the dead, leaving the tomb empty. One day he will return. That is a simple outline of Christian faith, the simplicity of the incarnation.

If we then ask about Jesus Christ's relation to the Father, we again have the answer of simple faith, that there is a personal threefoldness in the one God. This is the simple belief in the Trinity.

The majority of Christians are happy in reciting the Creed as their "head" belief, and trusting in their "heart" in Jesus Christ as their Saviour, their Lord, and their God. This book is concerned with the first, but does not shut its eyes to the second. Faith has two aspects, for the head and for the heart, and the two ultimately belong together. We are not called to believe within a vacuum.

As I have implied in the Preface, in these days many Christians want some sensible assurance that their faith makes sense, and in this book I want to show that it does. I am not trying directly to answer various modern objections by which some theologians have unsettled simple believers. We have nothing against an intellectual approach to Christian truth. Indeed this book is an attempted vindication of clear thinking, since I believe that the simpler Christian faith can be shown to make good sense for those who think it out.

Thus the reader will not find here arguments for or against modern theologians, quoting one against another. It may be said that my theologising is of no more value than that of some of these modern thinkers who have swung away from the old traditions. What I am trying to do is to plead the cause of the old faith on the ground that it can be shown to be sensible. There is no reason why some of the ancient words in the creeds (for example *substance*) should not be brought up to date, or certainly explained in modern terms, but since they summarise the New Testament teaching they must be explained, rather than explained away, to fit modern concepts. Once we start chipping away at one major item, such as the resurrection or the virgin birth of Jesus Christ, the whole edifice collapses. All that is left is for each person to argue how best to patch up the gaps in the building.

Obviously, you must judge whether I have been able to make out a sensible case for what you already recite in the creeds, or find impossible to accept.

If a man will begin with certainties,
he will end with doubts;
but if he will be content to begin with doubts,
he shall end with certainties.

Bacon: Advancement of Learning

CHAPTER 1
WHAT JESUS SAID OF HIMSELF

A man named Jesus lived and died in Palestine some two thousand years ago. It does not require faith to accept this. It is a fact of history.

Jesus became known as the Christ, which means the Messiah, whose coming had been foretold in the Old Testament. It requires faith to identify him in this way, and the New Testament tells how his first followers came to have this faith. It has formed the faith of the Christian church ever since.

There is one further step of faith, a big one, namely that Jesus the Messiah was also truly God. There had been, and have since been, men and women who are vehicles for the living power of God, but Jesus Christ is not simply different in "quantity" but actually different in "quality" since he was, and is, God himself.

This is the simple faith in the incarnation. Jesus is both truly God and truly Man. Hundreds and thousands of Christians have accepted this simple, profound statement, and have acted upon it by appealing to Jesus

Christ as the living God today. "Lord, save me" is as meaningful today as it was to Peter sinking in the sea (Matthew 14:30).

This is a good faith to live by, but does it bear thinking out? This is, of course, the whole theme of this book, but we must obviously begin with what we know of Jesus from the Gospel records. There are no other details of his life, and both ordinary Christians and also profound theologians have no other information to build on.

Each of us can therefore check a theologian's statements about Jesus by referring to the Gospel records. No theologian has a private line to God so as to learn anything fresh about the life and teaching of Jesus, or to find authority to reject anything that the Gospels record, unless a sceptical mind finds the authority in itself to regard something as unlikely or impossible.

It may sound a weak beginning to point out that Jesus did not announce that he was God. Some regard this as proof that he did not regard himself as God incarnate. It is worth noting that the writers of our four Gospels, who wrote for Christians who certainly worshipped him as divine, resisted the temptation to put divine claims into the mouth of Jesus. Their restraint in this way is a mark of the credibility of their writings. They might have wished that Jesus had been more explicit, but they were too responsible to write in claims that he did not make, although they themselves had come to hold them.

If Jesus had travelled round asserting "I am God", we should have known that he was nothing of the kind. His whole mission would have been futile, since it would have been impossible to establish a day-by-day working relationship with a group of disciples. The thought of his Godhead would have overwhelmed them, and inhibited all that they did.

Since, as we believe, Jesus was in fact God as well as man, he acted as one would expect God to act. As Longfellow wrote, "Though the mills of God grind slowly, Yet they grind exceeding small." Jesus moved slowly, one step at a time, with his followers.

As Jews, they believed in the coming of the Messiah one day, so Jesus fostered their awareness that he was the Messiah, or Christ, whose coming had been told beforehand in the Jewish Bible, our Old Testament. This was not easy, since there were at least three pointers to the Messiah in the Old Testament, and it must have been difficult to see how they could be brought together in one man.

There was no doubt that the Messiah was to be of the line of David, descended from David himself. There had been no king of David's line for over five centuries, but the prophecy of Isaiah, spoken while the descendants of David still had a century and a half to rule, had indicated that the line would become like the stump of a felled tree; but from this stump the great ruler would grow one day (Isaiah 11:1).

Similarly, in the last days before Jerusalem fell to

the Babylonians, Ezekiel declared that God would make a ruin of the royal house "until he comes whose right it is; and to him I will give it" (Ezekiel 21:25-27). Even when many of the Jews returned after the exile they did not have a king; and under the domination of Persia, Greece and Rome, the house of David was indeed reduced to a stump, and the Messiah was born in the humblest circumstances.

Another strand was the Messiah as one who would come from heaven. In Daniel 7:13-14, Daniel records a vision that was given to him. "Behold, with the clouds of heaven there came one like a son of man, and he came to the Ancient of Days, and was presented before him.

"And to him was given dominion and glory and kingdom ... his dominion is an everlasting dominion, which shall not pass away ..." However Daniel may have understood the figure of the Man, there is not the slightest doubt that Jesus identified the Man of the vision with himself, and indeed brought about his own condemnation by doing so.

When the high priest adjured Jesus by the living God, "Tell us if you are the Christ, the Son of God," Jesus replied, "You have said so. But I tell you, hereafter you will see the Son of man seated at the right hand of Power, and coming on the clouds of heaven." (Matthew 26:63-64).

Previously Jesus had told his disciples, "They will see the Son of man coming in clouds with great power and glory." (Mark 13:26). The high priest recognised that Jesus was claiming to be the Messiah when he quoted the Daniel verse of himself. But how was this claim to be reconciled with the prophecy of the Messiah from the line of David?

The third strand appeared even more contradictory, and thus was overlooked. This was the picture of the humble servant of God who would suffer and die for the sins of the world, even though he himself would be sinless. Christians are familiar with these Servant passages, which are found in Isaiah 42:1-8; 49:1-7; 50:4-9, and culminate in the incredible passage, 52:13-15, 53:1-12, describing the significance of his death after appalling ill treatment. "He grew up ... like a root out of a dry ground ... he was wounded for our transgressions ... and with his stripes we are healed ... the Lord has laid on him the iniquity of us all ... They made his grave with the wicked and with a rich man in his death, although he had done no violence, and there was no deceit in his mouth..." All the passages need to be read to get the full impact of the prophecy.

It seems to me impossible to read them without seeing that they refer to an individual, and that individual is Jesus Christ. Jesus said before he went to his death, "This scripture must be fulfilled in me, 'And he was reckoned with the transgressors'; for what is written about me has its fulfilment." He is quoting from Isaiah 53:12. (Luke 22:37).

Jewish interpreters regarded the Servant as representing either the nation in exile or a group within the nation. But elsewhere in the Old Testament the nation is regarded as guilty, and both Ezra, Nehemiah and Daniel confess the joint sins, not the innocence, of the people (Ezra 9, Nehemiah 1; Daniel 9). There is no indication anywhere of an innocent nucleus who were put to death as a sacrifice for the sins of the whole nation.

There is a similar group of passages in Zechariah chapter 11 and 13:1 where the good shepherd is rejected and put to death, with the result that a fountain is opened to wash away sins. Indeed, in Zechariah 12:10 the NEB and the margin of RSV give the alternative Hebrew (not Christian) reading "they shall look on ME whom they have pierced" ("me" instead of *him*) thus identifying the sufferer with Jehovah, the speaker. Neither here nor in Isaiah is this figure described as the Messiah, although the preceding context in Zechariah 9:9 speaks of the coming king who rides humbly on a donkey. The above words of Zechariah 12:10 are quoted of Jesus Christ in John 19:37 (at his first coming) and Revelation 1:7 (at his Second Coming).

Thus the third strand introduces a Messiah who is humble and ordinary, who is himself without sin, but who gives his life to take away the sins of others. While the first two strands describe rule over enemies, this strand identifies the essential enemies as the inner and outward sins of mankind. This is the identification made in announcing the birth of Jesus. "You shall call his name Jesus, for he will save his people from their sins" (Matthew 1:21).

Jesus was born as a Jew, and not a member of some other nationality or religion, because the Jews had been prepared for their Messiah, although they did not know when he would come. Jesus therefore began to build up in his disciples the realisation that he was the promised Messiah, and eventually drew from Peter the great confession, "You are the Christ [Messiah], the Son of the living God" (Matthew 16:16). This established a bridgehead, and indeed it formed the essence of Peter's preaching on the Day of Pentecost. "God has made him both Lord and Christ [Messiah], this Jesus whom you crucified" (Acts 2:36).

Once the disciples had the faith to say to the man whom they had known so well, "You are the Messiah," they were ready for the next step. What was the nature of the Messiah?

Although Jesus did not say "I am God," he said other things about himself which began to have fuller significance after his resurrection. For example, what did the title "Son of God" convey when he accepted this in Peter's confession? What did he mean when he claimed, "No one knows the Son except the Father, and no one knows the Father except the Son" (Matthew 11:27; Luke 10:22)? In what sense could he claim to be the final Judge of mankind (Matthew 7:22-23; 25:31-46)? And how could he himself forgive sins, when the bystanders rightly recognised this as a divine prerogative (Mark 2:5-7)? And who but God could promise what Abraham, Isaiah or Socrates could never say, "Lo, I am with you always" (Matthew 28:20)?

We have used quotations from the first three gospels, since some scholars believe that the Fourth Gospel, ascribed to John, has written in, and written up, what Jesus really said. The sensible alternative is that John had a more mystical temperament, and consequently retained these deeper inner teachings of Christ which the other writers passed by in their concern to record the practical teaching and actions which are of equal importance. Surprisingly enough, although John himself in his prologue gives his own belief that "the Word was God" (John 1:1), he does not put any such claim directly into the mouth of Jesus.

What he does record are statements of the same order, as we have seen in the other Gospels. They are statements whose implications have to be thought out. Thus "I and my Father are one" (John 10:30), "I am the Son of God" (10:36), "I have come down from heaven" (6:38), are certainly remarkable claims but could stop short of "I am God." At the same time mature consideration in the light of total experience may well lead to the interpretation that wrung from Thomas the cry of "My Lord and my God" (20:28), a title that Jesus did not reject when it was offered to him.

So at the time of his resurrection, there were a number who were prepared from their knowledge of him and his teachings to say, "This is the Messiah, the Son of God."

After his resurrection, Jesus taught his disciples

more about himself over a period of forty days (Acts 1:1-3). During this time we can be sure that he took them a step further in explaining the fuller meaning of this Messiahship. It may still have been difficult to say directly to his disciples, "I am God," but at least he moved their thoughts very far in this direction without lessening the reality of his manhood. Some would have grasped the truth more clearly than others, for Matthew says that they worshipped him, though some doubted (Matthew 28:17).

One hard barrier to surmount, since the disciples were monotheistic Jews, was naturally the relationship between the Father and himself. How could they easily say, "You are God" when there is only one God, and he in heaven? The belief in the Trinity needs a chapter to itself, but meanwhile we notice the relationship of three divine Persons in the command to baptize in the name of the Father, the Son and the Holy Spirit (Matthew 28:19), and in the association of the Three in God's coming to the people of God, "Another Counsellor to be with you for ever ... I will come to you ... My Father will love him, and we will come to him (John 14:16-23).

Without being irreverent, I want to take the analogy of a detective story. The story opens with a crime – only of course ours opens with the very opposite. There is a murdered body in a locked room, with the key in the door on the inside and the windows barred. Who was the murderer?

There is no reason why the author should not declare at once, "The butler did it." The story is then meaningless and unacceptable. Who was the butler? Why did he want to murder his master, and how did he manage it? The bare statement, "The butler did it," is useless.

The writer knows this. He uses the book to build up a case, and if he is a good writer and plays fair everything falls into place. We know at the end who the butler was, and why and how he did what he did. In other words, the fact was there from the beginning, and needed to be unfolded. The test of the solution was that everything made sense. One is reminded of the Bellman in Lewis Carroll's *Hunting of the Snark* with his assertion, "I have said it twice ... I have said it thrice: What I tell you three times is true." This was not the way that Jesus used to convince his disciples of his Godhead. He did not strain human relationships by saying abruptly, "I am God." But in everything he said and did, he provided the clues which could be interpreted in only one way.

"Where were you when I laid the foundation of the earth?"

Job 38:4

CHAPTER 2
"BEFORE THE WORLD WAS MADE ..."

These words appear in the prayer of Jesus on the night of his betrayal. The full sentence reads, "And now, Father, glorify thou me in thine own presence with the glory which I had with thee before the world was made" (John 17:5).

So Jesus declares that he was personally alive before he was born into the world. In other words, his birth was no ordinary birth in which a human being comes alive for the first time, but it was *incarnation*, a new life in which his already existing life took on genuine human existence. As the Christian hymn says, "He came down to earth from heaven."

This incarnation is not reincarnation, and Jesus was careful to add "before the world was". We cannot discuss reincarnation here, but those who accept it cannot of course go back beyond the original creation of the universe. Yet Jesus knew that he was living "before the world was".

There are two significant facts in Jesus' prayer. One is that heaven was his home before his birth on earth. The other is his special relationship with his Father. There is the simplicity of heaven above, as in the children's hymn:

> "There's a Friend for little children
> Above the bright blue sky."

Those of us who sang this hymn regularly as children found it simple and satisfying. This is not surprising, since the hymn has Jesus Christ on its side. When he prayed the prayer from which we have quoted, he "lifted up his eyes to heaven" (John 17:1). At his baptism, he had seen "the heavens opened and the Spirit descending upon him like a dove" (Mark 1:10). And when he withdrew finally from his disciples "he was lifted up, and a cloud took him out of their sight" (Acts 1:9).

For Jesus, and therefore for us, heaven is above. But as the hymn says, it is "above the bright blue sky". The Hebrews did not suppose that God was located in the upper atmosphere. Like ourselves they knew that the word *heaven* had several uses.

It could stand for the atmosphere in which birds fly (for example Genesis 1:20, Psalm 104:12, where the Hebrew word translated "air" is "heaven", as is the Greek "the birds of the air" in Matthew 6:26). It could stand for the distant sphere of the stars and other heavenly bodies (for example Genesis 1:14; Deuteronomy 1:10).

Finally, it could stand for the centre where God rules, and this is not confused with either of the other two; his throne is in his holy temple in heaven, which is "above earth and heaven", beyond them in the fullest sense (for example 1 Kings 8:27; Psalm 11:4; 148:13).

The naive objection to this concept of heaven as being above is that what is *up* in Britain is *down* in Australia. This is as stupid as looking at a globe of the world and concluding that since we walk upright, Australians must walk upside down. I happen to have been in Australia, where I still prayed to God above!

We must be clear what *above* means. It represents *away from* this world, and wherever one is on the world's surface *above* is *away from*. Heaven is not on earth. If it were, the Lord's Prayer would not make sense. "Our Father, who art in heaven … Thy will be done on earth as it is in heaven" (Matthew 6:9-13). Until the end of history there will be a distinction between earth below and heaven above.

It is not enough to say that heaven is where God is. The upholding life of God is present in, and with, the whole of his creation, animal, vegetable and mineral, for "in him (Christ) all things hold together" (Colossians 1:17; Hebrews 1:3). The theological term for this presence is *immanence*. Although we pray to our Father in heaven and may look upwards, we do not need to shout, since he hears us where we are. And yet this presence does not make this earth heaven.

Heaven is the state, or sphere, or dimension, where God is central and where he is obeyed absolutely. Any glimpse that the Bible gives of heaven shows a multitude of angels around the central throne of God, ready to do what he commands. Above all, they are continually praising him (for example Psalm 103:19-20; Isaiah 6:3; Revelation 7:11-12).

This praise of God needs a comment. One can caricature it by supposing that God created a crowd of flatterers who would continually be telling him how wonderful he is. In fact, the praise of God is best seen in terms of drawn-out response. The nearest comparison would be the response that is drawn out of us as we gaze at some amazingly beautiful scenery, or listen to some great piece of music. This is surely the way in which we shall praise God for all eternity, and may begin now, as we "praise him for his mighty deeds; praise him according to his exceeding greatness!" (Psalm 150:2).

When the Lord's Prayer is finally answered in all its particulars, then like John in Revelation 5:13 we shall hear "every creature in heaven and on earth ... saying, 'To him who sits upon the throne and to the Lamb be blessing and honour and glory and might for ever and ever!'"

Returning to the definition of heaven, we used the terms "state, sphere or dimension". These are quite inadequate, but are probably the nearest we can come to describing something that we cannot comprehend while we are in our present bodies. These terms imply that heaven is not a material place, for example on one of the far distant planets or stars.

A belief in a material heaven has sometimes led to ridiculous conclusions. I remember reading some time ago that it was possible to fix the distance of heaven from earth. If Christ travelled to heaven at the speed of light at his ascension, and on arrival sent the Holy Spirit back to earth, also at the speed of light, heaven must be five light days away from earth, since Pentecost came ten days after the ascension. Thus heaven could be looked for at a distance of approximately 80 billion miles from earth.

In spite of what may seem to be a naive view, one can sympathise with those who cannot hold the concept of "state, sphere or dimension" as an adequate view of heaven, and look upwards to the distant galaxies as our future abode. All that one can say is that the new heaven and earth will fit our new resurrection bodies.

We began by discussing the heaven where Jesus Christ was before his human birth, and we find every reason to regard it as above. This links on to several statements that Jesus made about himself. "I am the living bread which came down from heaven" (John 6:51). "I have come down from heaven, not to do my own will, but the will of him who sent me" (John 6:38). "I came from God and now am here. I have not come on my own; but he sent me" (John 8:42. NIV). "I came from the Father and have come into the world" (John 16:28).

Although these quotations all come from one Gospel, there are phrases in the other Gospels that are significant, although less conclusive; for example "The Son of man *came* ... to give his life as a ransom for many" (Matthew 20:28). "I *came* not to call the righteous, but sinners" (Mark 2:17). "I *came* to cast fire upon the earth" (Luke 12:49). (Emphasis added in all three verses.)

Moreover, this coming of Jesus Christ from heaven to earth forms a vital part of the early Christian faith in the New Testament. For example, "Though he was rich, yet for your sake he became poor" (2 Corinthians 8:9. Also Philippians 2:7; Hebrews 2:9; 1 Timothy 1:15).

We have spent some time on this section, since it is necessary to remove one of the superficial objections to our conception of Christ as coming to earth from heaven above.

"No one knows the Son except the Father, and no
one knows the Father except the Son and any one
to whom the Son chooses to reveal him."

Matthew 11:27

CHAPTER 3
THE SON AND THE FATHER

Some theologians dislike any attempt to "describe" God,
to make theological statements about him. They feel that
such statements treat him as a subject to be analysed.
Obviously we can hardly begin to understand him, and
yet he has told us in the Bible as much as we can
comprehend, and we shall be defeating his purposes if
we shut our eyes to what he has revealed, and leave him
as what the Athenians regarded as "An Unknown God"
(Acts 17:23).

So we turn to the revealed fact of Three Persons in
One God. Outsiders ridicule the doctrine of the Trinity,
and speak as though the church invented it to make
things difficult. "Three in One and One in Three" is
supposed to be too ridiculous to be taken seriously,
especially when the so-called Athanasian Creed, printed
in the Anglican Book of Common Prayer, piles definition
upon definition, including "In this Trinity none is afore,
or after other: none is greater or less than another; but
the whole three Persons are co-eternal together: and co-

equal. So ... the Unity in Trinity, and the Trinity in Unity is to be worshipped."

Presently we shall be discussing the whole subject in detail, but on the principle of removing superficial objections before we start, we note that there is at least one analogy of the Trinity in Unity, which we take for granted without seeing any difficulty in it.

This is the analogy of three-dimensional space, consisting of length, breadth and height. We cannot dispense with any one of the three, since they are a trinity in unity. Nor can we say that one is greater or less than another. There is also a very similar analogy in past, present and future as constituting time.

Christians approach the doctrine of the Trinity in several different ways once they are convinced from Scripture that the orthodox definition is the proper way of bringing together what God has revealed about himself. Some begin with the Three Persons, and face the difficulty of Unity. Others begin with one God and find difficulty in Three Persons.

Some visualise Persons as individual people. Others tend to think in terms of a vague Spirit. One problem, of course, is our desire to visualise where we cannot be content with statements as statements. Probably we shall have to be content with some compromise between the two. Obviously, in thinking of the almighty God we are bound to use analogies and pictures, as the physicist has to do when he tries to show the structure of the atom or the cell.

Later we shall give the Scriptural passages from which our belief in the Trinity is drawn. Meanwhile we take up the prayer of Jesus in John 17:5, "the glory which I had with thee before the world was made." We have seen that he had a life in heaven before his human birth. But the verse also refers to his particular relationship with God the Father.

Here we can go outside of John's Gospel to Matthew 11:27, to a very remarkable statement by Jesus. "No one knows the Son except the Father, and no one knows the Father except the Son and anyone to whom the Son chooses to reveal him." In his parallel passage Luke has "who the Father is ... who the Son is ..." (Luke 10:22).

This passage, added to the words in the prayer, speaks of a unique relationship of the Son with the Father. It lifts Jesus Christ at once from the category of a created being. In other words, if we can take the words of Jesus seriously we cannot regard him as equivalent to an angel or other spiritual being, any more than we can equate him with a great prophet when he was on earth.

It is true that some have identified him with Michael (which means "Who is like God?") the archangel (Head of the angels) in the Old Testament. This is the view of Jehovah's Witnesses, who in this way accept his pre-existence without admitting his Deity. The Seventh Day Adventists also regard *Michael* as his pre-incarnation name, but do not deny his Godhead.

Among other words of Jesus which bear on his relationship with his Father, there is the striking statement in John 10:30: "I and the Father are one." The word *one* in the Greek is neuter, and not the masculine which would mean "one person". Even so, the context shows that the Jews regarded the sentence as a blasphemous claim to be God (John 10:33).

In the prologue to his Gospel, John speaks of the relationship in different terms. "In the beginning was the Word, and the Word was with God, and the Word was God" (1:1). *Word* sounds impersonal but John goes on to make it clear that this Word was personally the agent in creation, and then became flesh and lived with his disciples as a human person (1:14). He is even more definite in the opening verses of his first epistle where he says that he and the other disciples saw, heard and touched the eternal Word of life who came from the Father (1 John 1:1.)

The Greek word for Word is *Logos*, which means more than what we think of as a single word from the dictionary. It carries the significance of meaningful *expression*. My words show what I am and what I intend. So John has in mind such passages as Psalm 33:6 ("By the word of the LORD the heavens were made") and Isaiah 55:11. ("My word ... shall accomplish that which I purpose"), while going back ultimately to the creative "God said" in Genesis 1.

John declares that "all things were made through him" (John 1:3), that is that the Word (Christ) was the agent of creation but did not act independently of the Godhead. Similarly Colossians 1:16 says that "all things were created through him and for him", and Hebrews 1:2 that through Jesus, God created the world.

The New Testament has more to say concerning Christ's relationship with God the Father. Thus Philippians 2:6 speaks of him as "in the form of God", ("in very nature God" NIV). Paul uses a word which means something more than superficial likeness. In fact, he is saying that Christ was fully God, and one can show that this was his meaning by verse 7, where at the incarnation Christ took the *form* of a servant.

The Greek word is the same as before. No one can deny that the form of a servant means that he became truly and fully man. Therefore the previous sentence must mean that he was truly and fully God. One could quote Hebrews 1:8 also, where Christ, unlike the angels, is called 'God' in a quotation that is applied to him from Psalm 45:6. The alternative translation in the RSV margin ("God is thy throne") is less likely in the context.

When he was on earth, Jesus spoke to God as Father. This certainly shows his true humanity. Like ourselves, he needed to live his life in openness to his Father in heaven, and we must discuss this later when we consider his divine and human natures.

Most Christians believe that the Father-Son relationship is eternal, although a few hold that the term Son does not apply until after the incarnation. The weight of the Biblical evidence, however, suggests that it is correct to speak of the eternal Sonship of Christ in the light of his natural use of the term "Father" as describing a unique and permanent quality of relationship. We have already noticed the remarkable statement in Matthew 11:27 that only the Father knows the Son, and only the Son knows the Father.

Other passages speak of God as sending his Son. Thus in the parable of the wicked husbandman, the owner of the vineyard "had still one other, a beloved son" whom he sent (Mark 12:6). In the well-known passage in John 3: 16-18 we read that God so loved the world that he gave his only Son, and sent the Son into the world. The adjective translated *only* (as most moderns) or *one and only* (NIV) certainly emphasises uniqueness. In KJV and RV it is *only begotten*, which is a literal rendering of the two parts which make up the Greek word *monogenēs* (μονογενής – pronounced *mon-og-en-ace*).

In the epistles, Romans 8:3 God sends his own Son, in Galatians 4:4 God sent forth his Son (a slightly stronger verb indicating sent out from heaven), in Hebrews 1:2 he has spoken to us by a Son in contrast to humans and angels. (RSV here preserves the literal Greek while other translations add "*his* Son.")

The weight of evidence, then, is on the side of prenatal and eternal unique Sonship. Later we shall have to consider other aspects of the title Son of God, as it is applied to Jesus Christ.

Assuming then that the word Son is rightly used of the relationship with the Father before his birth, what does it signify? This is one of the great stumbling blocks for Islam. Neither Mohammed nor modern Muslims can accept the idea that God can beget a son, and the removal of the difficulty may have influenced the changing of the translation *Only begotten* to *only* in John 3:16 (RSV).

Muslims and some others find it impossible to separate sonship from the physical act by the father. Hence, we must make it clear that the word in the context is a strong picture word of an existing relationship, without pressing it to refer to origin. If one wants to venture beyond this, we can say that if the title *Father* is a proper eternal title for God, then it would be meaningless unless there was an eternal *Son*. While there is much in Scripture, as we have seen, to show that Christ had a life in relationship with the Father before he was born on earth, there is never a hint that he had a beginning, or that God actually became a Father. Thus he *became* man, but never *became* God.

The Father-Son relationship is probably the clearest picture that we can have of a relationship that we can never comprehend, since God is infinitely beyond our human understanding. The difficulty is greater for visualisers, as many of us are. Unless we can have a picture in our minds of the two Persons, we cannot be happy. And often we continue to build on the picture, and draw conclusions from it which go beyond what is legitimate.

If, then, we use the term "begotten", as our creeds do, we must realise that it is intended to rule out the creation of the Son. Thus we say "begotten, not created," and "begotten of his Father before all worlds, God of (from) God," in an attempt to avoid overmuch visualising.

Yet why criticise a simple mind, looking up into the sky and picturing an old man with a beard sitting on a throne, and his son beside him? He is seeing what is essentially true, and this is the only way in which he can visualise. After all, this is very much what Daniel saw in Daniel 7:9-14 and John in Revelation 4 and 5.

"The worldwide Christian faith is this: that we worship one God in Trinity, and Trinity in Unity." (The so-called Creed of St Athanasius in the Book of Common Prayer).

CHAPTER 4
THE TRINITY OF THE BIBLE.

The relationship of Father and Son inevitably raises the fact of the Trinity. Is it a complicated concept of Christian philosophers, or is it the truth that God has shown us about himself in the Bible? Christian thinkers during the first centuries assumed the latter, and they set to work on the Biblical material in the same way as a scientist sets to work on the material in the world around him.

The purpose of both is to formulate certain conclusions which will henceforth form guidelines for living. Many people will be happy to take for granted the guidelines on facts. Others would like to check them for themselves.

In the field of science it is possible to reach anti-scientific conclusions by seizing on one or two facts while ignoring others, for example the flat earth theory. Some early Christians did the same with theology. Thus by selecting texts, some concluded that the One God played three different parts at three different times, like an actor. Indeed, the Greek and Latin words for Person could mean the part played by an actor.

Others concluded that if Jesus Christ was Son, there must have been "when he was not" , that is he was not from eternity, and hence was inferior to the eternal Father.

Although the complete New Testament revelation of the Trinity was accepted either consciously or unconsciously quite early, it took three or four hundred years for a formula to be agreed which would be a guide to Christian thinking.

This formula was set down in the creeds and definitions which all the main churches, Catholic, Orthodox and Protestant (whether Episcopal or Free Church) have accepted as their official statement of belief. This has been possible only because the definitions can be demonstrated from Scripture as a whole.

We must see, then, how the Christian belief in the Trinity is grounded on Scripture, which means that it comes through the revelation from God himself.

We can state the conclusions simply:

The Deity of the Father
This is taken for granted all through the New Testament, and no one would dispute it.

The Deity of the Son
We have already considered the Gospels, especially the acceptance by Jesus of Thomas's cry addressed to him, "My Lord and my God" (John 20:28). One cannot treat this as a pious exclamation, since the Jews did not use

God's name in this way.

Turning to what the New Testament writings say about Jesus Christ, we look again at John's statement in John 1:1. "The Word was God," the Word being Jesus Christ, as the context shows (verse 14). Jehovah's Witnesses argue that the Greek word for "God" here does not have the definite article, as it often does, and that therefore the true translation should be, as in their New World Translation, "The Word was a god."

Apart from the fact that *theos*, God, varies over its use or lack of the definite article (for example it is without the article in vs.12-13,18) there is a regular rule in Greek that the predicate which follows the verb "to be" in the third person, is distinguished by the omission of the article, whatever the order of the words may be.

Thus the Greek writes, "The fear of the Lord is beginning of wisdom." So although John writes the four words in reverse order, "God was the Word," we are bound to take "the Word" as subject, and "God" as predicate because of the omission of the article.

We have already noticed the inescapable parallelism in Philippians 2:6-7 where "the form of God" is the same word as "the *form* of a servant". If the second means full manhood, the former must mean full Godhead.

The New Testament writers have no hesitation in coupling the name of Jesus Christ with the Father, and even giving him the precedence in "The Grace of the Lord Jesus Christ, and the love of God ..." (2 Corinthians 13:14).

Translators are divided over Romans 9:5. The Greek may be rendered as (RSV) "... is the Christ. God who is over all be blessed for ever," but RSV admits in the margin, "Christ, who is God over all, blessed for ever." The NEB is similar.

There is far less ambiguity in a similar ascription in Titus 2:13. Here RSV has "the appearing of the glory of our great God and Saviour Jesus Christ." This is certainly the most natural translation of the Greek words, and the RSV margin is very much a second best, "... of the great God and our Saviour Jesus Christ." Moreover, while the New Testament speaks of the appearing and coming of Jesus Christ, it nowhere speaks of the appearing of God as constituting the Second Coming. This of course is a matter of terminology and not of fact.

One can tell what a person believes not only by what he says but by what he obviously takes for granted when he makes a statement. In particular, we note the casual quotations which identify Jesus Christ with Jehovah.

Thus John 12:40-41 says that Isaiah's vision of Jehovah in Isaiah 6 was a vision of Christ himself. Similarly Revelation 2:23 applies to Christ words of Jeremiah 17:9-10 which say that Jehovah is the stone on which men stumble, and in 1 Peter 2:7-8, the verses are quoted of Christ. In Hebrews 1:10-12, Christ, like Jehovah in Psalm 102:25-27, is the Creator. Jehovah makes the absolute claim in Isaiah 44:6, "I am the first and I am the last; beside me there is no god," and this claim is made by the risen Christ in Revelation 1:17, "Fear not, I am the first and the last."

Someone said very wisely that the Deity of Jesus Christ is like the salt in the sea. You do not prove that the sea is salt only by the dried crystals on the shore, but by the saltiness of every drop of the ocean. Similarly the Deity of Jesus Christ is carried in solution by nearly every page of the New Testament. To put it another way, the New Testament would lose its heart if Jesus Christ were not God.

The Deity of the Holy Spirit

The Holy Spirit is both God and personal. Thus, when Ananias and Sapphira lied about the amount of a sale which they were giving to the Christian community, Peter told them that they had lied to the Holy Spirit, and immediately followed by telling them that they had lied to God (Acts 5:3-4).

The Holy Spirit is inextricably linked with the Father and the Son when Paul says, "There are diversities of gifts, but the same Spirit; and there are varieties of service, but the same Lord; and there are varieties of working, but it is the same God who inspires them all in every one" (1 Corinthians 12:4). There is also the well-known Grace in 2 Corinthians 13:14, "The grace of the Lord Jesus Christ and the love of God and the fellowship of the Holy Spirit be with you all."

We find it hard to think of the Spirit as personal, but although emphasis is laid on his power in action, this is not impersonal power. Thus "the Holy Spirit said, 'Set apart for me Barnabas and Saul for the work to which I have called them'" (Acts 13:2). The Spirit has an understanding mind to help us in our prayers (Romans 8:27). We are told "Do not grieve the Holy Spirit of God" (Ephesians 4:30). All these verses thus describe him as having personal qualities, and thus being himself personal.

It is worth noting that often the Greek words for the Spirit and the Holy Spirit have the definite article when the emphasis is on his personal being, whereas the omission of the article calls attention to his influence and power, for example Acts 1:5 without the article "You shall be baptised with Holy Spirit" and 1:8 with the article, "When the Holy Spirit has come upon you."

Distinction between the Three
This appears at the Baptism of Jesus, when Jesus came up from the river and the Holy Spirit descended upon him from heaven accompanied by the Father's voice (Mark 1:11). On earth, Jesus prayed to the Father (John 17) and promised that the Father would send the Holy Spirit (John 14:26). Naturally, if one took these texts by themselves, one might conclude that there were three Gods.

Unity of the Three
Distinction of person and activity must be balanced by unity. Thus the presence of One is the presence of All.

The Father did not become man, but "God was in Christ reconciling the world to himself" (2 Corinthians 5:19) and "through the eternal Spirit Christ offered himself without blemish to God" (Hebrews 9:14). The Spirit of God in the heart of the Christian means Christ in the heart (Romans 8:9-11). There is a beautiful sequence in John 14:16-23, where the coming of the Spirit to indwell is the coming of Christ himself, as well as the coming of the Father. NEB "We will come."

This is the evidence of the Bible. If it is true, the only simple conclusion is that God is both One and Threefold. We do not say that it is simple to comprehend God, but Christians have found a wonderful simplicity in approaching the Three in One. As Paul says in Ephesians 2:18, "Through him [Christ Jesus] we have access in one Spirit to the Father."

We ought to make it clear that each of the Persons is the centre of a special activity. The Father did not become man, but the Son did. The Holy Spirit came to fill the church and the individual. Yet the total Godhead, as we have seen, was involved in every activity.

Similarly, Christ was the divine agent in creation. "All things were created through him and for him" (Colossians 1:16), "All things were made through him" (John 1:3). Yet the Father also was involved. "Through whom [Christ] he created the world" (Hebrews 1:2). And the Holy Spirit also. In the beginning "the Spirit of God was moving over the face of the waters" (Genesis 1:2), "When thou sendest forth thy Spirit, they are created"

(Psalm 104:30).

One might find an analogy in ourselves. When I eat my breakfast, my body is the centre of my activity. When I sit in my chair and think, my mind is the centre of my creation of ideas. Yet my body is "human me" and my mind is also "human me", that is I am one person with at least two centres of personal activity.

Our God, heaven cannot hold him,
    Nor earth sustain:
Heaven and earth shall flee away
    When he comes to reign.

Only his mother,
    in her maiden bliss,
Worshipped the Beloved
    with a kiss.

Christina G Rossetti

CHAPTER 5
THE VIRGIN BIRTH

In this chapter I want to show that if one believes in the incarnation, one is bound to believe the physical fact of the virgin birth. There are only two accounts in the New Testament of the conception and birth of Jesus Christ. They are found in Matthew 1:18-25 and Luke 1:26-38. Both are obviously entirely independent of one another, and both say that Jesus was conceived of the Virgin Mary without a human father. There is no other description of how he came to be born. If we argue for any alternative we can only do so on subjective grounds, and not on any alternative historical evidence.

Although these are the only records, it is clear that other New Testament writers also believed in the virgin birth. Thus Mark, who does not begin his Gospel until the start of Christ's ministry, indicates the virgin birth in

Mark 6:3. The parallel passage in Matthew 13:55 quotes onlookers who said, "Is not this the carpenter's son?" while Luke 4:22 quotes "Is not this Joseph's son?" Matthew and Luke could not be misunderstood after their record of the virgin birth. Mark, on the other hand, simply records the words, "Is not this the carpenter, the son of Mary?" thus omitting any reference to Joseph as his father. In the arguments of the moment, it is likely that all three expressions were used, and all three evangelists are correct.

John also implies a knowledge of something suspicious about the birth of Jesus when he quotes the words of the Jews in John 8:41: "*We* were not born of fornication" (emphasis added.) The insertion of the pronoun "we" in the Greek, when the Greek verb by itself would normally be sufficient, gives emphasis, and a contrast with Jesus himself.

There is also an early variant of John 1:12-13, which has the singular instead of the plural, which would be a clear reference to the virgin birth. Although very few scholars accept this reading, the NEB cleverly leaves the interpretation open when it reads "... he gave the right to become children of God, not born of any human stock, or by the fleshly desire of a human father, but the offspring of God himself."

Paul also is seemingly aware of the virgin birth. When he writes of the birth of Abraham's sons in Galatians 4:22-24, he uses the word *gennao* which has overtones of the father's act. When he writes in 4:4 that

Jesus Christ was "born of a woman" he uses a much more general verb, *ginomal*, which denotes coming to be. He uses the same word of "descended from David" in Romans 1:3 (NEB uses "born"). Paul and Luke were travelling companions, and Luke in his opening verses says that he had taken the greatest care over checking his sources. It would have been surprising if they had not met Mary in Palestine, and Luke, as a doctor, would have been especially concerned with her story, and Paul would also have accepted it.

Yet the virgin birth did not form part of the preaching of the disciples, presumably because of their respect for Mary's reputation which could have been talked about unfavourably among unbelievers.

So the record of Jesus' birth is simple, with the same simplicity as we find in the Christian Christmas cards and hymns that both children and adults enjoy. But how far is the fact simple? We go back to what we have already seen: God became Man. This was the deliberate action of one who was, and is, personal. This is seen in such a passage as Philippians 2:5-10, where he deliberately empties himself of his glory. Nothing less than this will meet the New Testament evidence.

Thus, we must say that Jesus Christ in Palestine had the same identity as he had as Son of God in heaven. If he genuinely became man he must be more than a supreme prophet, a man totally filled with the Spirit of God. There were godly prophets in the Old Testament, but none were incarnations of God.

If he were not God in person, the atonement would be robbed of much of its meaning, for God would have stopped short of personal ultimate involvement in the supreme sacrifice. The burden would have been shouldered by someone else, even though that someone was his nearest and dearest.

On the other hand, he could not be *only* God and *not* man. Probably some of the appearances of the angel of the Lord, who speaks as Jehovah in the Old Testament, were temporary manifestations of Jesus Christ; for example Genesis 16:7,11,13; Exodus 3:2,4,7. He may well have been the one who wrestled with Jacob as he was crossing the river in Genesis 32:22-32.

These were not incarnations, inasmuch as they did not make Christ a member of the human race. Yet from the beginning of man's creation, Christ had left open the possibility of incarnation. Man, and man alone, was made in the image of God (Genesis 1:27). This implies that God could become man but could not become any other creature. Hinduism with its many animal gods thinks differently.

So Christ's incarnation involves two things. He must retain his identity as God, but he must also undergo human birth – which alone could make him a member of the human race. That is the simple fact and there is no possible alternative, provided we believe that God became Man.

How, then, could these two things come about? It would not be sufficient for Christ to lay hold of a human being in the manner of a possessing spirit, for this would not make him a member of the human race. Incarnation had to be by the gateway of conception and birth from a human mother. But it could not come through the agency of a human father, since human father and human mother produce a potential person from the moment of conception, a person of body, mind and spirit. If Christ personally could somehow squeeze into such a person, the result would be two different persons in one, a concept which the Christian church has always rejected on the basis of the Gospel records.

Some have evaded a miracle by speaking of *parthenogenesis*. This is a technical word which means *virgin birth*. It is used of some insects, when the female produces young without mating. The common greenfly on the roses is an example during part of the season. The worker bees in a queenless hive are a better example for our purpose. The queen normally mates only once, and can then lay eggs to produce workers, which are female, in which case she inseminates them with the sperm which her body holds from the drone with which she mated.

To produce drones (males), she lays eggs without inseminating them. If the hive loses its queen, some of the workers are able to lay eggs, but since these are unfertilised they can produce only drones. So the male drone carries the chromosome of femaleness.

With humans, the reverse happens. Every cell in the body, with one exception, consists of 23 matching pairs of chromosomes which are carriers of genes, which lay down the basic characters of one's life. At conception, the male and female sex cells unite their respective chromosomes, and thus create one new life which is a blend of the two. The determination of the sex of the new child comes as follows: among the chromosomes there is one that determines maleness, and in a human being this is carried only by the man, and is known as the Y chromosome.

I spoke of matching pairs of chromosomes, but in fact one pair in the man is paired X and Y. The corresponding pair in the woman is X and X. If at conception the ovum in the female is fertilised by a Y, the child will be a boy. So, if in some way a mother were to produce a baby without fertilisation, the child would inevitably be a girl because she has no Y chromosome. If Mary had somehow experienced a freak parthenogenesis, Jesus would have been a girl.

We have singled out the sex chromosomes to make our point, but this is only a small part of the story. Chromosomes carry the genes which play a large part in determining what we are to become. They are like building blocks, and each set is exclusive to ourselves. They determine the materials of the building of our life, but do not determine the use we make of them.

Each cell of a normal body, with one exception, contains 23 pairs of these matching rod-like chromosomes, 46 in all. The whole body is built up by the constant division and multiplication of the cells, but the

46 chromosomes are retained because of the way in which the division is made. Before multiplication of the cell, each chromosome divides down its length and the halves become two cells, each of the proper 46.

There is one exception, and one can easily see what this is. If the sex cells in man and in woman, like all the other cells, each had 46 chromosomes, after fertilisation there would be 92 chromosomes, and these would of course double again and again with fresh marriages. So the chromosomes of the sex cell divide in a different way. Only one of each pair of chromosomes goes into the new cell, so that now the sex cells of man and woman each have only 23 chromosomes. At fertilisation the full number of 46 is restored once more.

All this may sound complicated, and since we are professing to be simple we must put the case very simply indeed. This is the mechanism by which you and I inherit from father and mother. I am one person (with 46 chromosomes in each cell) but I am of two natures (23 from my father, 23 from my mother). Thus I have certain capacities and certain ways of looking at things because I have my father's nature, and other capacities and ways of looking at things because I have the nature of my mother. So the phrase, "one person and two natures" is a simple statement of what *we* are. We shall meet the phrase again in a more significant sense when we consider the incarnate Person, Jesus Christ.

It may at first seem irreverent to pry into the genetics of the virgin birth, but since it is often rejected on scientific grounds, we must say honestly what is involved in the virginal conception. Incidentally, when we speak of the virgin birth we are actually concerned with the virginal conception, although the official belief of the Roman Catholic Church is that the birth itself was miraculous and left Mary a *virgo intacta,* so that a medical examination would have shown her still to be a virgin.

The Second Person of the Trinity chose to become Man, not merely to resemble a man, but to become a full member of the human race which he had created. He had to be born, but he could not force his way into someone else's baby already conceived with its 46 chromosomes. There is only one simple solution, although it could not possibly have been understood by the New Testament writers. They wrote what they knew to be history, and recorded the birth of Jesus Christ from a virgin.

It is left to us with our modern knowledge of genetics to see that this is the only way by which the Second Person of the Trinity could become a member of the human race. Through the 23 chromosomes in the ovum in Mary's body, Jesus became a member of the human race. These chromosomes were the end products of the line of David and of many others beside, going back ultimately to the first true man and woman.

The other 23 chromosomes must have been contributed by the miraculous act of God to be the vehicles of the personal being of the Son of God. We note what the

Bible has to say, "She was found to be with child of the Holy Spirit ... That which is conceived in her is of the Holy Spirit" (Matthew 1:18,20). "The Holy Spirit will come upon you, and the power of the Most High will overshadow you; therefore the child to be born will be called holy, the Son of God" (Luke 1:35).

These are quotations from the RSV and other translations, but it would not be pedantic to point out that in all three passages in the Greek there is no definite article before "Holy Spirit". We have seen as a frequent rule, especially in Luke's Gospel and Acts, that the definite article calls attention to the Person of the Spirit while its omission emphasises his work in action.

A good example near the beginning of the Gospel is Luke 2:24,26-27. It is said there of Simeon that "Holy Spirit" was upon him, he was inspired as a prophet. Moreover, "it had been revealed to him by *the* Holy Spirit ... and inspired by *the* Spirit he came into the temple" (emphasis added).

Matthew and Luke both omit the definite article in writing of the virginal conception. An obvious reason for this is to avoid any entanglement with paganism. Pagan mythology was full of stories of gods and goddesses who had sex relations with humans, the children then being heroes of antiquity, like Hercules. Hence the use of the definite article might convey to the pagan mind the idea that God actually had physical relations with Mary. In fact this is what Muslims imagine that Christians teach in speaking of Jesus Christ as the Son of God.

What both Matthew and Luke have conveyed is that Holy Spirit action brought about the miraculous birth. This is enforced by the phrase in Luke 1:35: "Power of the Most High will overshadow you," where there is again no definite article before "power". Luke removes every idea of physical relations without removing God's miraculous action.

We have seen that a cell of 23 chromosomes had to be supplied, if a cell of 23 within Mary's ovary was to be fertilised. This cell must contain the Y (or male) chromosome. Since we are facing a miracle, corresponding to the miracle of the resurrection at the end of Christ's life on earth, there is no possibility of saying how this cell was formed. We can only say that, under the creative and formative power of the Holy Spirit, the cell was formed which could be the vehicle of the personal life of the Second Person of the Trinity.

It has been objected that Luke's record of the angel's words, "Therefore the child to be born will be called holy, the Son of God," represents a different theology from Paul's description of the Son of God from heaven. This of course is one of the exasperating objections from theologians who do not think back to realities. How could Mary at that stage have grasped "Pauline theology"?

She was told the simple truth in words that would make sense to her. She was to be the mother of the Son of God. The full meaning of this could come later, without producing any contradiction.

Note 1: Descent from David
Although the genealogies in Matthew 1 and Luke 3 both appear to be Joseph's, one must be Mary's if Jesus Christ was to be physically, and not merely legally, of David's line, as the prophets and the angel had said. Several solutions have been suggested, but one is reasonably simple, along the lines of Jewish law.

We know that Mary had a sister, since John 19:25 says, "Standing by the cross of Jesus were his mother, and his mother's sister, Mary the wife of Clopas, and Mary Magdalene." At first sight one might read this as though Mary's sister was Mary the wife of Clopas, but this would not be possible, since both sisters would not have the same name of Mary. There is no mention of a brother in the Gospels.

If we assume that the genealogy in Luke 3 is Mary's, then her father would have been Heli. Yet Heli here is the father of Joseph. Since there were no sons, Joseph would become legally the son of Heli on his marriage, so as to preserve the family name and inheritance. We read of this rule in Numbers 36, which shows us why Mary had to marry a man who was also descended from David. Thus Jesus was the son of David, both legally through Joseph and physically through Mary.

Note 2: Ephesians 4:9
There is a probable reference to the reality of the incarnation in this verse, although it is generally overlooked. The words "he had descended into the lower

parts of the earth" are often taken as referring to Christ's descent into Hades. It seems more likely that Paul has the words of Psalm 139:13-15 in mind, where David compares the darkness of the womb to being "intricately wrought in the depths of the earth". Thus Paul says in Ephesians that Christ came to earth and was formed as a baby in the darkness of the womb in order that he might win the victory, and return to heaven as conqueror with the captives that he had delivered.

This does not deny Christ's descent into the realm of the departed, but this passage is not one to support the fact, as does 1 Peter 3:18-20. The subject is discussed in another chapter.

Note 3: Theotokos
Many years ago a clergyman friend of mine found himself in difficulty when chairing a Protestant meeting. One of the speakers was attacking Roman Catholic devotion to the Virgin Mary. In particular he objected to her description as Mother of God. At once, a group of Roman Catholics began to chorus, "Do you deny the hypostatic union?" The unfortunate speaker did not see the point, even if he knew that *hypostatic* meant *personal*. But the chairman was a theologian, and he had to intervene on the side of the Roman Catholic objectors. He knew that *Mother of God* is a possible translation of the Greek word *Theotokos (Θεοτόκος)*, to which orthodox Christians are committed by its use in the Chalcedonian Definition of AD 451.

The problem of the translation of the word *Theotokos* has never been adequately solved. The Greek word is made up of two basic words, *God* and *child-bearing*. The word was introduced to indicate that the child born of Mary was God from the beginning. He was not a purely human child to Whom the Godhead was later added, thus producing two persons, a divine and a human. *Mother of God* might suggest that Mary originated the Godhead. *God-bearer* might suggest that she was purely the receptacle of the Godhead.

Note 4: Jesus Christ and original sin

Original Sin is not a phrase that occurs in the Bible, but it is a useful term to express our experience, namely that there appears to be something in us from our beginning, or origin, which inclines us to do wrong. Since this could not be by the direct creative action of God, the evil twist is naturally connected with the post-creation fall, and since it occurs in every human being it must be handed down from parents to child. Since, then, Jesus Christ was born of Adam's race, how could he have been exempt from original sin and thus be free both from original and from actual sin?

Roman Catholics have a logical solution in the doctrine of the Immaculate Conception of the Blessed Virgin Mary, if it is properly understood and not caricatured. Her body was conceived in the normal way, but her soul from the moment of its existence was so sanctified by God's grace that she, at the centre of her being, was free from original sin. For original sin lies in the absence of God's sanctifying grace, which is a concept that we shall discuss later.

If we do not accept the Roman view, some suggest a miracle of grace which did not allow original sin to operate in the miraculous conception. An alternative suggestion that original sin is transmitted through the father, and not through the mother, has not commended itself to most Christians.

We must go deeper. So far we have spoken of original sin almost as though it were original naughtiness, concerned only with doing what father, mother, aunt or society decides is bad for us and for them. But sin lies in our attitude to God. Although we are born with the life of nature, we are without the eternal life that comes through being reborn by the Holy Spirit of God (John 3:5-6; 1 Corinthians 2:10-16; Romans 8:9).

Unfortunately, "religious" thought often holds that every person has eternal life within, and that the way of salvation is to bring out this life of God by meditation, right thinking, right action, or by other ways. Texts that are quoted in proof are always texts that in the New Testament apply only to those who have become Christians through trust in Christ, and through the action of the Holy Spirit who has come in to dwell in the centre. Nowhere in the New Testament is it suggested that we become Christians by letting out, or developing, something that is already within.

Life, that is eternal life, the life of God himself, is

God's gift from above. Although it is everlasting in quantity, the primary emphasis is upon its God-quality. It is not an insurance for unending existence that is independent of God himself.

St John's Gospel is one of the finest life tonics that there is, and chapter 5 is one of the clearest. There we read that "as the Father has life in himself, so has he granted the Son also to have life in himself" (26). Jesus adds, "You refuse to come to me that you may have life" (40). And an earlier verse speaks of our having eternal life and of having passed from death to life (24).

Since, then, Jesus came not only to give us an example of living, but to give us what we lack by nature, it follows that we are born without this life of his and hence are without the inner link with God. Lack of this inner link is that which ultimately will turn into actual sin, which is turning from God and his will. Hence original sin is, negatively, a non-relationship with God, and without that relationship we cannot lift ourselves, by ourselves, to attain it and rise into eternal life.

Once we see this, we see, however dimly, how Jesus Christ could be fully human and yet free from original sin. If original sin is the lack of life, Jesus Christ is himself THE LIFE, and could not be conceived or born out of relation with LIFE. While we enter LIFE through being reborn, Jesus Christ had no need to be born again.

A further note on how this affects the temptations of Jesus is at the end of Chapter 6.

> The very God! I think, Abib; dost thou think?
> So, the All-Great, were the All-Loving too –
> So, through the thunder comes a human voice
> Saying, "O heart I made, a heart beats here!
> Face, my hands fashioned, see it in myself."
>
> *Robert Browning: An Epistle of Karshich*

CHAPTER 6
GOD BECOMES MAN

So far, we have seen a simple pattern. The Second Person of the Trinity, fully God and hence eternal, chose to become subject to time as a full member of the human race, so that he might redeem us from sin and pour his eternal life into us. To achieve this he had to be conceived by a human mother, but he could not cease to be the person that he had always been. Hence the orthodox Christian belief has always been that Jesus Christ, since his incarnation, is both God and Man. However difficult this is to visualise, it forms a simple sequence of thought.

Jesus Christ was fully human as we can see from the Gospel records, and many people would not go beyond this. His body was human, and had the same needs as our bodies have. He needed food and rest. He suffered pain to the acutest extreme in his trial and death on the cross.

One vital part of the human body is the brain, with which we acquire knowledge. So we are told that "Jesus increased in wisdom and stature" (Luke 2:52). Yet, if God knows everything, how could Jesus increase in wisdom? One might use an analogy. When a building is to be erected, the architect knows the whole of it before it is begun. The builders learn the building piece by piece as they work on it. If the architect became one of the builders, he would also gain a step-by-step knowledge of it. After the incarnation the divine architect became also a human builder, and experienced the life of the world as a vital participant.

One of the apparent problems is really a very small problem indeed, although it is thrown up against the Christian faith by members of the sects like Jehovah's Witnesses who deny the Deity of Jesus Christ. It concerns the prayers of Jesus. In praying to God, was Jesus praying to himself?

In becoming human, Jesus took up a fresh relationship with his Father in heaven. It was a relationship of human dependency, and this involved prayer. Since we need to pray, he too needed to pray to the Father to whom we pray. This was an essential factor of his humanity, as essential as was food to sustain his body.

A Christian, then, believes fully in the complete humanity of his Lord. There is, however, something more to say about humanity. When Jesus Christ became Man was he simply an individual unit? There are two well-known sayings that come from John Donne (1572 -

1631), "No man is an island, entire of itself." And, "Any man's death diminishes me, because I am involved in Mankind. And therefore never send to know for whom the bell tolls; it tolls for thee." This concept will be strange and difficult for some Christians; so since the emphasis of this book is on simplicity, we must use some illustrations that make sense.

First, there is the fact of telepathy. Although we cannot explain it, very many intelligent people accept it as a fact. Quite apart from the dull statistical evidence that has been produced in laboratory tests, most of us can tell examples of one person becoming aware of the danger of a friend in another part of the world.

There are other more ordinary occasions of awareness that seemingly go beyond the range of the senses, sight, hearing, and touch. Some people have this sensitivity as a fairly regular experience, while others may have it on rare occasions and often as no more than a vague feeling. The simplest explanation is that there is a linkage of some sort that on occasions can be opened up.

Without introducing Spiritualism, there are some people with what we will call clairvoyant capacities who seem to "know" the minds and doings of people who otherwise are total strangers. It is as though we are all part of a telephone system to which we are all involuntary subscribers, and we can at times be rung up.

There is another experience which we may call the linkage of the group. Our interests draw us to others with similar interests. One has only to see the specialist magazines on a bookstall to realise the extraordinary number of groups that there are. One cannot say that this is simply a matter of units coming together with a common interest. There is a spirit of fraternity, or sorority that is felt among the members and the group becomes almost a living society. The society becomes effectively linked to other similar societies, like cells in a body.

Today we hear much about the one world and its needs, and we are continually seeing our oneness with others who are superficially very different from ourselves. It may well be that there is a total bond corresponding to a soul of humanity.

Each of us probably belongs to more than one group, concerned with such subjects as football, cricket, bowls, ornithology, stamps, history, archaeology, cars. I have deliberately omitted the group that forms the Christian church, since although there is the natural group link here, there is the deeper link of the Holy Spirit who forms us into the Body of Christ.

We shall be considering this higher factor later. But the natural group feeling comes out in an exaggerated form in some aspects of church life, where members are over-conscious of denominational loyalties, or even of particular theological emphases, which override unity in Christ. Thus Protestants and Roman Catholics have unchurched one another, and writers on the Second Coming have treated almost as enemies others whose interpretations of this event differ from theirs.

All these examples are intended to illustrate what one may accept as a fact of human existence. The body of humanity is made up of many parts. Each part, like the physical body, has its own system, but each system is part of a greater whole – which one can call the soul of humanity in which every human being is bound to share.

We must apply this concept to the incarnate Lord Jesus Christ. We have established that you and I are not like the bricks in a house, but like cells in a body. When Christ became man he became an integral part of total humanity, linked to all other members of the human race. Thus it is said of him, "He knew all men and needed no one to bear witness of man; for he himself knew what was in man" (John 2:25).

This does not mean that he was consciously thinking of every single human being all the time. Our extended awareness that we have spoken of is not constant. God has made us so that we normally live in the conscious world of the senses, and we assume that Jesus lived like this.

Yet as we have seen, the world of consciousness may open up so that one becomes aware of people or happenings beyond the range of the normal senses. Jesus, being perfect man, was able at will to open the normally closed gate and become aware of an individual or group of his fellow men. Thus he surprised Nathaniel by telling him that he saw him under the fig tree when he was alone (John 1:48).

If we think it out, this concept of total inner linkage throws considerable light on the incarnation and atonement. If Jesus Christ had been no more than a single unit, he would not have been fully part of the soul of humanity. His death on the cross could have atoned perhaps for one other unit only. But if, like ourselves, in becoming man he became one with the body and soul of humanity, then he could carry humanity with him to the cross. He was not "an island, entire of itself".

This may well be the place to draw the distinction between forgiveness and atonement[*]. One of the objections thrown up against Christians sounds so simple. "If I forgive anyone without asking for an atonement, surely a good God should do the same!" The answer is that if God had not first had this extent of forgiveness, he would not have become incarnate. "God so loved the world that he gave ..." (John 3:16). God had already done as much as we can do. In fact, he had done more.

You and I generally wait for some signs of apology and reform. But as Paul points out, "One will hardly die for a righteous man – though perhaps for a good man one will dare even to die. But God shows his love for us

---

[*] Publisher's footnote: The atonement in Christian terms is the reconciliation of God and humans brought about by the redemptive life and death of Jesus. Its use in this paragraph refers to reconciliation between people.

in that while we were yet sinners Christ died for us" (Romans 5: 7-8). One cannot fault God over his forgiveness. Our trouble is that we cannot blot out the sin.

God needed to do more than pronounce "I forgive", although he could do this in the Old Testament times in anticipation of what he would do through Christ in the future. "In his divine forbearance he had passed over former sins," in Old Testament times (Romans 3:25). If a mere declaration were sufficient, why should incarnation be needed?

God was concerned with the dynamic restoration of the human race. Since the human race could neither restore itself nor be restored by word of command, God became a member of the race, so that although sinless, he could pay the penalty of its fallenness by taking it to death on the cross – for all humanity was taken with him to death on the cross when Christ bore the sins of the world. Thus there followed forgiveness, cleansing and, above all, restoration into fellowship with God. This is a change that no ordinary human forgiveness could bring about. We cannot take away sin, whether our own or another's, but "the blood of Jesus his Son cleanses us from all sin" (1 John 1:7).

I would make another suggestion about the true manhood of Jesus, with which all Christians will not agree. It is often argued that his miracles are a proof of his Deity. Certainly they are a proof of his Messiahship, since they had been foretold and hinted at in the Old

Testament, as Christ himself pointed out in a synagogue service (Luke 4:16-21).

But nonetheless they may still be regarded as the actions of the perfect man. It is probably true that every one of Jesus' recorded miracles can be paralleled by similar miracles done through men of God in the Old Testament (not to mention those that are recorded in Acts), even the apparently miraculous awareness of Nathanael's actions (John 1:47-51). Elijah and Elisha restored the dead to life (1 Kings 17:17-24; 2 Kings 4:32-37), multiplied food and liquid (1 Kings 17:14-16; 2 Kings 4:42-44) and healed the sick (2 Kings 5).

Thus in Jesus we see capacities that would be found in unfallen man, including the commonly unrecognised "miracle" of riding an unbroken colt through the excited Passover crowds (Mark 11:1-10). Man was given control of the animal world (Genesis 1:28).

We are, of course, referring only to the miracles that Jesus *himself* performed. The two supreme miracles of the virginal conception and the resurrection are regarded as miracles done *for* him. The virginal conception is through the action of the Holy Spirit (Luke 1:35), and the resurrection is the act of the Father (Acts 2:32; Romans 10:9; Galatians 1:1; 1 Peter 1:21). While Jesus performed miracles, including raising the dead, he is never said to have raised himself from the dead.

We have spoken of Christ's Messiahship, and in Chapter 1 we noticed that Jesus was concerned to have this accepted by his disciples. Once they had believed in him in this way, they were in a position to ask what the Messianic claims of Jesus involved.

The titles and relationship involved in the words Son of God are developed as the New Testament unfolds, until we see the final revelation of the eternal sonship. We have also seen that Mary was able to grasp that since her child was to be conceived through the direct action of God, he would be the Son of God (Luke 1:35). The same title has a meaning for Mary, and a fuller meaning for us. There is no contradiction, as some have supposed, between the ideas of Matthew, Luke and Paul, but only an expansion.

There are passages in the Old Testament which connect the title with Messiahship. The most prominent of these is Psalm 2:7 where the Lord declares of his chosen king, "You are my son, today I have begotten you." The verse cannot mean that the king has been born on that very day. Rather it means that this is the day of proclamation, appointment and recognition, probably even the day of anointing, for the term *Messiah* in Hebrew, like the equivalent *Christ* in Greek, is primarily a title meaning *Anointed*.

In fact the title Messiah, Anointed, is used of prophets, priests and kings in the Old Testament, although obviously in most instances it would be misleading to translate it as "Messiah", even though features of prophets, priests and kings emerge in Jesus the Messiah. Indeed, the title is used only once specifically of the future Messiah. This is in Daniel 9:25-27, where an anointed (Messiah) prince is cut off and makes an end of the sacrifices, although even this application to Jesus is disputed by many modern commentators. But by the time that Jesus was born, all Jews were looking for the special Messiah of David's line (John 7:42).

To return to Psalm 2, it is possible to interpret it in highly pictorial terms of David, or another ruling king, facing the threat of attacks on his people. On the other hand, the verses are quoted of Jesus Christ in Acts 4:24-27, and certainly they appear to have a wider view than the throne of a Jewish king.

The verse from Psalm 2 that is singled out for special quotation in the New Testament is verse 7, "You are my son, today I have begotten you." This is quoted of Jesus Christ in Hebrews 1:5 and 5:5. We are inevitably reminded of the similar declaration of Sonship in the words from heaven at the baptism of Jesus, "This is my beloved Son, with whom I am well pleased."

There were Christian interpretations in the first centuries that saw the baptism as the begetting of Jesus as the Son of God through the entry of the Holy Spirit. Thus it was held that Jesus became the Son of God when he was filled with the Spirit of God at his baptism. Similarly, the anthroposophist Rudolf Steiner held that the cosmic Christ descended on Jesus at his baptism. This would not be a true incarnation, although it might be rather more than the filling of a prophet when he was inspired by the Spirit of God.

The baptism of Jesus was indeed his designation as

the Messiah, the Son of God, anointed to fulfil all that had been foretold of the coming King in the Old Testament. Previously Jesus had not taken up his Messianic task, but had grown up as an ordinary member of family and community.

There followed the time of temptation in the wilderness. Sometimes this has been interpreted as a time of uncertainty in his mind as to whether he was indeed the Son of God. This is understandable if Satan's words are taken in one sense, namely "*If* you are the Son of God" (Matthew 4:3, emphasis added). But "if" can stand for "since" in an argument of absolute certainty. Thus we might say, "If two and two are four, three twos must be six." And obvious use of the word in this sense is in Romans 8:31, "If God is for us, who is against us?"

Christ's replies to Satan show that the temptations were to use his divine powers in the wrong way. Thus the temptations concerned the true way of being the Messiah, the true life of the Son of God on earth.

To sum up, the title Son of God is meaningful in more ways than one:

1. The eternal Son in relationship with the eternal Father.

2. The one born of the Holy Spirit in union with the Virgin Mary.

3. The Messiah fulfilling the divine prophecies of the Old Testament.

4. The resurrection was the final declaration of his title on earth (Romans 1:4).

Each of these aspects is worked out in the New Testament without the slightest contradiction.

Note: How was Jesus tempted?
There are two significant passages in Hebrews. The conclusion of chapter 2 is concerned with one of the results of true incarnation. "Since therefore the children share in flesh and blood, he himself likewise partook of the same nature" (Hebrews 2:14). "Because he himself has suffered and been tempted, he is able to help those who are tempted" (verse 18). The other passage is 4:15. "We have not a high priest who is unable to sympathize with our weaknesses, but one who in every respect has been tempted as we are, yet without sin."

This is the simplicity of the incarnation, although we perhaps naturally tend to complicate it by asking, How could God be tempted? If we read Hebrews 2:18 again we can see that he had the temptations that flesh and blood are heir to, and 4:15 adds *all* the temptations. But how could anyone, even Jesus Christ, experience every single temptation that has come to every single person who has ever lived?

First of all, the words translated "tempt" and "temptation", both in Hebrew and Greek, have to do duty for the two meanings "test" and "trial". This distinction was not made in the Authorised Version (KJV), but modern versions bring out the two meanings. An obvious example is Genesis 22:1, where the KJV says that God tempted Abraham, while the RSV more correctly translates "God tested Abraham." In fact, Satan tempts to make us fall, whereas God tests in order to strengthen, yet the Hebrew and Greek verbs are the same.

Another clear example is James 1:2-3, where "various trials" (KJV "divers temptations") produce stronger faith, while in 1:13 God tempts no one, the context speaking of enticement to evil. When there were discussions in the Church of England about revising the wording of the Lord's Prayer, in place of "Lead us not into temptation" we were given "Do not bring us to the time of trial," a more meaningful translation. But the pressure of tradition proved too strong and the words were changed back again.[*]

Insofar as temptations are trials, there is no difficulty in seeing that Christ suffered all the sorts of trials that are common to mankind. In Luke 22:28 he says to his disciples, "You are those who have continued with me in my trials." His trials included tiredness (Matthew 8:24; John 4:6), intense hunger (Matthew 4:2), and thirst as he waited for water from a well (John 4:7), and his agony when he hung on the cross.

But temptations go further than trials, and are enticements to do what is wrong. Earlier I said that Satan tempts, and I mentioned the record of Christ's temptations, two of which are introduced by the words, "If you

---

[*] Publisher's footnote: "Do not bring us to the time of trial." This wording has now come into widespread use, and is also the wording in some recent Bible translations.

are the Son of God," intended to persuade Jesus to take the easy way. To turn stones into bread to satisfy his acute hunger would be to use his divine powers for himself, whereas during the whole of his life he never worked a miracle for his own benefit.

The words thrown at him on the cross had more meaning than the mockers realised: "He saved others; he cannot save himself" (Matthew 27:42). Another temptation was to throw himself from the top of the temple and count on angels to carry him safely to the court below. This would test his divine powers and set him on the path of winning followers through spectacular means, instead of by the quiet methods that his Father had called him to adopt.

Finally, Satan offered to withdraw his power over mankind in favour of Jesus – if Jesus would simply recognise his sovereignty and perhaps go into partnership with him. Thus Jesus would gain the kingdom without the agony of the cross. Indeed, Satan used this last temptation again on a later occasion when through Peter he urged him not to consider a violent death (Matthew 16:21-23). We can adapt these temptations to ourselves in lesser measure, since Jesus Christ was tempted as we are.

Yet we must go further. We are reminded in James 1:14 that temptations also come from within. "Each person is tempted when he is lured and enticed by his own desire." If Jesus Christ was sinless, how could he be enticed by evil from within, by original sin? None of us can enter into Christ's inner experience, so we can only speculate about these inner promptings to do wrong. Could he really be tempted in every respect as we are, yet without sinning (Hebrews 4:15)?

A suggestion has been made, which I do not follow myself, but mention it for consideration: The actual Greek words in Hebrews 4:15 are "apart from sin", and "yet" is not there. Hence it has been suggested that the meaning is that Jesus Christ was tempted so far as one who was without original sin could be. We need not adopt this interpretation, but we must not exaggerate the force of original sin in pulling us into doing wrong.

If we take the example of an alcoholic, he has an overwhelming urge to take drink after drink. Christ certainly did not have such an overwhelming urge. But if we go back to the very first drink, the future alcoholic had no powerful urge on that occasion. It was as easy for him to say No as to say Yes. He could easily resist the temptation, and almost certainly it was not the smell and taste of the drink that attracted him, but the pressure of his friends. Jesus deliberately said No on every first occasion.

Probably most of our powerful temptations are the result of habit formation after an easy beginning. We can imagine that Jesus Christ intelligently said No on the first and subsequent occasions, and thus did not know the pull of evil habit. He recognised his Father's will. There was one recorded occasion when his body tried to assert itself over this will. In Gethsemane the awful realisation of the coming cross caused him the most terrible agony (Matthew 26:38-39; Luke 22:41-44). Christ was no robot, computerised to go to the cross. His body cried out for a way of escape, but in the end he submitted to his Father, "not my will, but thine, be done." There is another comment on this in Hebrews 5:7-9.

To sum up; although Jesus did not go through every single temptation that has come to me today, he was tempted along all the same channels as myself. His temptations are not simply of academic interest, and we remind ourselves of one of the verses with which we began. "Because he himself has suffered and been tempted, he is able to help those who are tempted (Hebrews 2:18).

The picture of a fly sitting deciding what it is going to make of an elephant has comic elements about it.

CS Lewis: What are we to make of Jesus Christ?

CHAPTER 7
JESUS CHRIST: GOD AND MAN

We now come to an aspect of the incarnation that cannot honestly be treated as simple. The reason is that the incarnation is unique. We can perhaps imagine God appearing in a materialised form, and we can certainly imagine a man completely devoted to God. But the New Testament gives us one who is both true God and true Man. If he is the same person who is one with the Father from all eternity, then he is truly God. If he is one with us, then he is truly man. This is summed up beautifully in Philippians 2:6-7, "Though he was in the *form* of God, [he] did not count equality with God a thing to be grasped, but emptied himself, taking the *form* of a servant, being born in the likeness of men."

The word *form* in Greek denotes essential being, and since the form of a servant means essentially man, who had been created to be the servant of the Father, the earlier use of the same word, "the *form* of God" must mean that he was truly and fully God. (Emphasis added in all verses.)

Because the concept of the God-Man is so difficult to imagine, Christians have tended to exaggerate the one against the other. With the best will in the world, Christians down the ages have tended on the whole to emphasise the fact of Jesus Christ as God. This is hardly surprising, since the incarnation is so marvellous, and is the ground of our salvation.

However, in modern times there has been a considerable drift the other way. The idea of incarnation has been played down, because it is too much for modern thought to handle. What has been suggested as an alternative is Jesus as having the values of God for us, or Jesus as perfectly displaying the character of God to us, or some other concept that avoids our having to say, "Jesus Christ is God." Yet, however difficult it is to conceive it, this confession is God's truth, and toning it down is error. Thus 1 John 4:2-3 declares unequivocally, "By this you know the Spirit of God: every spirit which confesses that Jesus Christ has come in the flesh is of God, and every spirit which does not confess Jesus is not of God."

In the content of John's first epistle we may note also 5:6, "This is he who came by water and blood, Jesus Christ, not with the water only but with the water and the blood." This is a puzzling verse, but I believe it has a straightforward meaning. We have already seen that some early Christians believed that the Christ entered into Jesus at his baptism, "with the water".

Since John is, as we have seen, arguing for the true

incarnation, it must be that this is contained in the words "the blood" and not simply with the water. Now when John wrote his Gospel, he spoke of conception as being "of blood" (John 1:13). Actually, the Greek is in the plural, "of bloods", referring presumably to the blood of father and mother coming together in the child. He says there that this is not the sort of birth that he is writing about. It is not the natural birth that we have experienced through fathers and mothers, but the new birth from God. In his epistle (1 John 5:6) he speaks of belief in the incarnation. If, as we wrote earlier, John knew of the virgin birth, he naturally uses the singular in his epistle here. The only blood is that of the Virgin.

We have noted that many Christians have tended to come down on the side of the Godhead of Jesus Christ, and this is certainly true of some devout believers who are suspicious of any emphasis on his humanity. Obviously they accept his humanity as a fact, but they cannot integrate it into their thinking. Hence they are puzzled by his temptations, since as God could he really and truly be tempted into sin?

As a mark of his Godhead, I have even heard one enthusiast assert categorically that Jesus knew everything that was going to happen during the day when he woke up in the morning. If this were true, it would only be an extreme example of the gift of prevision which certain people enjoy spasmodically, and is no proof of Deity.

Whence did he derive his teaching? The indication is

that when he taught, he had the clear conviction that he was saying what he had come to say on the authority of his Father. Because he was so completely one with his Father, and no sin came between, he could not help but speak the words of God. "The Father who sent me has himself given me commandment what to say" (John 12:49). Thus what he said carried all his Father's authority (John 14:10; 17:14). In this way he showed, "I and the Father are one" (John 10:30).

How far does this help in understanding Christ's statement that he was ignorant of the date of his Second Coming, although this was known to his Father (Mark 13:32)? Since this was a secret completely hidden from angels and humans alike, it was hidden from the Son who had become man. If he had asked, What will be the date? his inner mind would have been totally unresponsive. But when he spoke as commissioned, he experienced the inner glow of "this is so". His Father's word coincided with his own.

We must therefore try to picture, as far as we can, what was involved in the day by day life of the One who was, and is, God and man. There is no need to do this if we are happy to know by simple faith that Jesus was both God and man, and are willing to leave the matter there. But if we believe that for honesty's sake we must go a little further, then we need some guidelines to help us.

How far was Jesus aware of being God as well as man? One cannot *be* something without at times knowing it, and earlier we have referred to sayings that indicate that Jesus knew he was God. But this does not mean that he withdrew in thought and action from the normal experiences of human living. We must be careful not to split Jesus into two compartments. Thus the Christian definition as, for example it is found in the Athanasian Creed as quoted in the Anglican Book of Common Prayer, is that Jesus Christ has two natures but is one person.

As a person he never drew on his divine powers to help himself. We saw this in discussing the temptation to turn stones into bread to satisfy his acute hunger. Yet he creatively multiplied the loaves and fishes to feed the crowds.

This use or non-use of his Deity sounds unreal at first sight. So let us come back to our own purely human experience. Many people today accept that below the level of our conscious brain there are deeper levels from which all kinds of experiences may emerge. At the simplest level there are the stored memories, some of which can be recalled at will, but the majority have gone beyond recall, although they can often be brought back in vivid detail under hypnosis.

Then there are inner forces which may affect our lives for good or evil. These are often referred to as repressions, and unlike deliberate suppressions they generally centre round some incident or enforced attitude in early life which the conscious mind has refused to recognise because they suggested guilt. But these repressions can emerge in dreams, using symbols whose disguise cheats the conscious mind, or they can set up unpleasant behaviour patterns and even physical illness.

If these things become too severe, the person may find help through a psychiatrist, who by suitable techniques will try to discover the source of the inner conflict. This is the emphasis of the Freudian school.

Psychologists of the Jungian school emphasise the inner forces that try for effective and creative expression. They are seen in the arts, and in many aspects of daily work where the person is not content to be a mere cabbage. Moreover, they help to make us more balanced in our character if we will let them. The fact is that our personalities open up in various ways. Thus we have the people who enjoy the inner world of ideas and often of mystical experience.

At the opposite end there are the down-to-earth realists, and others who are essentially activists. So we have the balance of the emotional and intellectual types, the authoritarians and the easygoing gentle types. One might continue classifying, but the point is that the shadow sides of our personality also try to find expression, although this is more and more difficult as we gradually harden into our set type.

As we saw before, the repressed shadows may emerge in symbolic dreams or even in uncharacteristic behaviour patterns. It may need assistance to admit the shadow in one's life, but theoretically one can see that a fully balanced man, who has allowed more than one aspect of personality to grow, is better than one who is personally compressed along certain lines. Yet however much we try to bring the shadows out, we shall always find that we are still experiencing one or two patterns of thought and behaviour more than others. The world and the church would be the poorer if we were all the same.

So under the surface, as it were, we have the level of memories that are recallable or un-recallable by the brain, and the level of dynamic forces that affect our behaviour and attitudes by way of repression or pressure.

Before going further, let us tentatively see what relevance this has for Jesus Christ. Undoubtedly he built up a store of memories as he grew up from childhood. We have only a limited recall of our memories, so it is hard to imagine that a perfect person could have complete recall whenever he wished. In fact Christ could recall the glory which he had with the Father before the world was made (John 17:5). So we can assume, by analogy with our human memories, that Jesus Christ could recall any memory if and when he needed it, or dismiss it from his mind for the time being.

There is no indication in the Gospels of any negative repression in Jesus' life, but what about the Jungian shadows? His behaviour suggests that there were none. In other words, he was perfectly developed in every aspect of personality. We can see this in the way he was absolutely at home with every type of person.

You and I often find ourselves on a different wavelength when we meet other people. Jesus was on every wavelength. Or to put it from another point of view, when we want help we go to Mr X, while someone else will go to Mrs Y. We single out the person who we know can help us. But everyone could go to Jesus. To quote again John 2:25, "He knew all men ... he himself knew what was in man."

There is a good example of this in his choice of his disciples, men of different types, but all knowing that he understood them. We may be thankful for this when we read the New Testament. Matthew, the legally minded tax gatherer, is interested to give us many down-to-earth laws of the kingdom.

John was probably the only one who was moved by the more mystical teachings. Moreover, it is noteworthy that Jesus was apparently at home with all women as they were with him. One can see this in the light of Genesis 1:27, "God created man in his own image, in the image of God he created him; *male and female* he created them" (emphasis added.) So, as God and Man, we should expect to find this oneness with men and women, and evidently with children also. It need hardly be said that in the Bible the translation "man", except in a male/female context, means a human being. A different word is used for a male person.

There is one further difficulty that some have found in the fact of the incarnation. The New Testament, as we have seen earlier, says that Christ was the creator of all things and "in him all things hold together" (Colossians 1:17). Moreover, Hebrews 1:2-3 similarly speaks of him not only as creator but as "upholding the universe by his word of power".

This brings us to what the Bible teaches about the nature of creation. When you and I make or create objects, they have a separate existence from ourselves. When we die, they remain as before. But God's creation of the universe is of such a kind that if, impossibly, God were to cease to exist, the whole universe would immediately vanish into non-existence.

This does not mean that the universe is a part of God, or that God is a part of the universe, which is the view known as Pantheism. But it means that the life of God is the energy which sustains everything in existence, whether it is mineral, vegetable, animal, or human, righteous, sinful, or without moral sense. This is more understandable today than when atoms were thought of as solid blocks. For now we know that the further we investigate the basis of the world, the more we discover that what we may tentatively describe as energy, is at the structure of everything in the form of protons, neutrons and electrons, all frantically on the move.

We cannot worship these mysteries as God, but Christ is using this energy force as a means of maintaining the universe in existence. The energy has its source in him. I am using the term *energy* as a popular and understandable term, and am not attempting to define it scientifically. Religiously, I see it as God's life force. At least we can say that nothing in the universe can maintain its existence apart from God.

Some theologians have raised the question of how Christ could still be upholding the universe when he was living as man. It has been suggested that he handed over the work to the Holy Spirit until his return to heaven. There is perhaps a simpler answer. What does this upholding involve? It need not involve a conscious running about the universe doing this and that. God gives us certain analogies with our own experiences.

Our bodies are sustained and upheld by an unconscious life force. We do not consciously control all that goes on within us, for example our digestion. A cut will instantly set forces in motion within the body to fight infection and bring healing. In fact, we normally have no control over most of the things that constitute our life. The life force is operative without our having to direct it deliberately. If the directing force whereby Christ sustains the universe is somewhat of this order, he does not have to be thinking about it all the time, even though it flows out from him.

Assuming that each one of us owes our existence to this force, we must be linked to each other by virtue of our sharing in the one life force. When Christ became truly man and a member of his own creation, he also naturally as man was involved in this life force in a new way. He was not detached from all that he had done in creation, but now he not only shared its inflow into his human body, but continued the outflow which had always been his. But as we have seen, membership of the divine life force does not involve a conscious effort either for God or for us.

Note: Two Natures, One Person.
Theologians in the early church struggled to find ways of defining the person of Jesus Christ. Words had differing meanings with different peoples, especially when definitions had to be transferred from Greek to Latin and vice versa. This was true of the terms to be used for the Trinity.

In Greek, *Ousia* was used for *real being*. The Son was of the same real being as the Father, that is fully God and of the same real being as ourselves.

Phusis was *nature,* and Jesus Christ was "in two natures ... as regards his Godhead, begotten of the Father before the ages, but yet as regards his manhood begotten of Mary the Virgin ... one and the same Christ, Son, Lord, Only-begotten, recognised in two natures, without confusion, without change, without division without separation ... the characteristics of each nature being preserved and coming together to form one person and ego, not as separated into two persons, but one and the same Son and only-begotten God the Word, Lord Jesus Christ".

This quotation from the Council of Chalcedon (AD 451) also introduces two Greek words which are equivalent to *person. Prosopon* and *Hypostasis.* Here, in default of any clear alternative to *person*, I have suggested the translation *ego*.

The main thing is to find a formula that preserves the unity of Christ's Person, while preserving his godhead and manhood. Allowing for older philosophic terms, one can see that this is what the Definition of Chalcedon, from which I have quoted, has done.

Members of the Church of England who use the Book of Common Prayer will find there a statement in the Athanasian Creed covering the same points as does the Chalcedonian Definition. It is best to treat this creed as a definition, without worrying about its over-emphasis on the absolute correctness of belief as necessary for salvation, although naturally one wants to understand what to believe.

In the Alternative Services Book the omission of the Athanasian Creed, at least its body of doctrine, is a sad loss. As a young boy I was always thrilled by its recitation on Trinity Sunday. I felt it truly revealed God in his wonder and majesty. I have since heard of others on whom this Creed had a similar enlightening effect in childhood.

Jesus said, "It is finished."

John 19:30

CHAPTER 8
THE CLIMAX OF THE INCARNATION

"Christ Jesus came into the world to save sinners" (1 Timothy 1:15), and the central point in that salvation was his death on the cross, where "God was in Christ reconciling the world to himself" (2 Corinthians 5:19). The Bible nowhere suggests that on the cross God was punishing an innocent man. The whole point of this book is to show that God himself, in the Person of the Son of God, became man in order to redeem us.

Sin has so many aspects. Thus it holds us in prison from which Christ redeemed us. Matthew 20:28: "The Son of man came ... to give his life as a ransom for many." Ephesians 1:7: "We have redemption through his blood." 1 Corinthians 7:23: "You were bought with a price."

The New Testament dwells on the picture of present freedom, and never names Satan as our captor, or anyone else, as one to whom money was paid to set us free. Only one or two points can be illustrated at a time by the pictures that are used, and the symbol of paying the debt that we have incurred through our sins is used without suggesting who receives the ransom money.

Again, sin brings us into God's court where we stand guilty before him. We cannot work off our guilt, but "the judgment following one trespass brought condemnation, but the free gift following many trespasses brings justification" (Romans 5:16). *Justified* means being entirely cleared in God's court, and "since we are justified by faith, we have peace with God through our Lord Jesus Christ" (Romans 5:1). Sin is something that demands atonement through the shedding of the blood of sacrifice, for which the Jews had been prepared in the Old Testament ritual laws. Hence Jesus Christ made atonement through his sacrificial death on the cross.

We are not saved by Jesus' good life alone, but his perfect life had to be terminated by the shedding of his blood. The term "blood" in this connection in the New Testament always refers to sacrificial death and never to his life. "Without the shedding of blood there is no forgiveness of sins" (Hebrews 9:22).

Sin is the breaking of God's law, and is more than letting ourselves down. It carries the curse of death upon it, which means ultimate execution. But Christ took the curse upon himself, when he died the form of death on which a special curse had been placed. This is worked out in Galatians 3:10-14; and Colossians 2:14 declares that Christ "cancelled the bond which stood against us with its legal demands; this he set aside, nailing it to the cross".

Sin also is the dirt from which we cannot clean ourselves. But "the blood of Jesus his Son cleanses us from all sin" (1 John 1:7). Sin is darkness out of which God has brought us into his light. "Once you were darkness, but now you are light in the Lord" (Ephesians 5:8). "Him who called you out of darkness into his marvellous light" (1 Peter 2:9). Again, sin is the state of enmity or rebellion against God, but Christ has reconciled us so that we enjoy friendship with God. "While we were enemies we were reconciled to God by the death of his Son" (Romans 5:10). "Our fellowship is with the Father and with his Son Jesus Christ" (1 John 1:3).

Each of these pictures may well be followed up, remembering that pictures cannot be drawn out beyond the essential point that they are illustrating. In particular, whatever picture we use, we must not draw the false conclusion that Jesus Christ was more loving than an angry Father. We cannot set one Person of the Trinity against another. The text to have in mind is 2 Corinthians 5:19: "In Christ God was reconciling the world to himself."

The New Testament is full of these pictures, each centred in the sacrificial death of the Lord Jesus Christ, God incarnate, on the cross. Similarly, the Old Testament carries the great predictive prophecy of Isaiah 53. "He was wounded for our transgressions, he was bruised for our iniquities; upon him was the chastisement that made us whole, and with his stripes we are healed. All we like sheep have gone astray; we have turned every one to his own way; and the LORD has laid on him the iniquity of us all" (Isaiah 53:5-6).

There is another important piece of evidence. This is the act of worship known variously among Christians as the Lord's Supper, the Holy Communion, the Eucharist, Divine Liturgy, the Mass, instituted by Jesus Christ to be a memorial of his atoning death. The striking thing is that this service, however much it was clouded over with extra doctrines, kept the atoning death of the Lord in front of both simple and sophisticated persons alike down the centuries.

Since this book is intended to help Christians in the church as a whole, I want to try to write helpfully about the significance which Christians of different traditions find in this service. There is an essential difference between Roman Catholic and Protestant teaching: Protestants emphasise the receiving of the symbols of the broken bread and poured out wine as token of salvation through the death of Jesus Christ.

Roman Catholics agree with this, but go further and offer the consecrated bread and wine as a sacrifice. They do this because they believe that the bread and wine are transformed into the body and blood of Jesus Christ (transubstantiation), and can be offered to the Father as the church's own sacrifice in and through Christ.

The term *Mass* has been used especially by Roman Catholics. Originally it was a Latin word, *missa*, *dismissal*, a word used in the conclusion of the Latin Mass. *"Ite, missa est,"* literally "Go, it is the dismissal", a command to take Christ out into the world, although there are several opinions as to the exact translation and meaning.

To the Protestant, the Roman Catholic belief seems to come near to repeating the sacrifice of Christ made once and for all upon the cross, although the Roman Catholics deny this. The Protestant points out that the New Testament, taken in its natural sense, speaks only of eating and drinking "in remembrance of me" and of the action as "proclaiming the Lord's death until he comes" (Luke 22:19; 1 Corinthians 11:25-26).

We cannot argue the two views here, beyond noticing that some Roman Catholics translate "Do this in remembrance of me" (1 Corinthians 11:24; Luke 22:20 margin) as "Do this for my memorial", and interpret the normal Greek word for "do" in a sacrificial sense, that is "Offer this for my memorial." Similarly, the proclaiming of the Lord's death is taken as proclaiming to God by presenting once again the sacrifice of Jesus Christ.

I have tried to set this out fairly, and one might add that belief in the actual presence of Christ in the elements (the consecrated bread and wine), without the full idea of transubstantiation, has been held by a number in the Anglican church, leading here also to the offering of the sacrifice of the Eucharist.

Among Protestants there is the simple remembrance of the benefits of the death of Christ, and until recently the Lord's Supper, which is the only term used in the New Testament (1 Corinthians 11:20), was almost an extra on a few Sundays. People would attend, say, on the first Sunday in the month.

Lately there has been a complete change in the Church of England, and the family service with Communion has often become the central service on Sundays. The symbols of the bread and wine are received not only in gratitude for the death of Christ, but also as "a participation in the body and blood of Christ" (1 Corinthians 10:16), and as a demonstration of union with our fellow Christians since "we all partake of the one bread" (1 Corinthians 10:17).

This has been a long, and yet only partially adequate discussion of the service which our Lord himself instituted at the Last Supper before his death.

There is another fact to add about the death of Christ. This is its effect on Satan and his hosts. Christ himself spoke of his coming death as the occasion when "the ruler of this world will be cast out" (John 12:31). Satan is spoken of as "the god of this world" (2 Corinthians 4:4), and in the temptation of Jesus he claimed the right to hand over the rulership to him (Matthew 4:8-9). The word *world* in this sense refers to the false system that governs so much of human life, and not to the earth with all its beauty.

Satan is evidently a fallen angel who though created perfect, rebelled against God and with others was cast out of heaven. We gather something of the nature of his fall by references in Isaiah 14: 12-20 and Ezekiel 28:11-19, where the king of Babylon and the king of Tyre are spoken of in more than human terms, which could well be an allusion to Satan. Thus the king says, "I will ascend above the heights of the clouds, I will make myself like the Most High" (Isaiah 14:14), and God says of him, "You were on the holy mountain of God ... Your heart was proud because of your beauty (Ezekiel 28:14,17).

The fall of man in the garden of Eden placed him on the same side as Satan, and gave Satan power over him. According to the story in Genesis 3, death was the result of human sin. Fossil remains show that death was in the animal world from earliest times, but now men and women were given the chance of being more than animals, and being sustained by the spiritual life of God in their animal bodies. Their fall meant a double death, once they cut themselves off from God. Dissolution began in their bodies, and their inner life also died. If mankind had not fallen, one can guess that in due time they would have been transformed to spiritual bodies without passing through death, as will happen at the Second Coming (1 Thessalonians 4:15-17).

When Jesus came, he died to impart the spiritual life of God once more, so that the believer "does not come into judgment, but has passed from death to life" (John 5:24). Moreover, although our bodies must die, the sting of death has been taken away, since Christ became flesh and blood so that "through death he might destroy [NEB:

break the power of] him who has the power of death, that is, the devil" (Hebrews 2:14).

Taken at its face value this surely means that we need not be frightened when we pass through the gates of death. If we are Christians we know that our sins have been taken away in Christ, and we do not go out into the darkness of the unknown.

But the New Testament, as well as we ourselves, knows that Satan is still active, as though he can get the better of God. We are engaged in a constant battle against "principalities, against the powers, against the world rulers of this present darkness, against the spiritual hosts of wickedness in the heavenly places". We need the defensive armour and the offensive weapons that Christ provides in order to conquer (Ephesians 6:10-18). From another angle, we read in Revelation 12:7-12 of Satan being cast down to the earth with his angels, where he is overcome "by the blood of the Lamb, and by the word of the Christians' testimony". So we are brought back once again to the marvellous power of the death of Christ on the cross.

We have written earlier of the inner link that binds all men and women and children, and we may think of this as equivalent to a soul of humanity. We saw that Jesus Christ at his conception was integrated into the human race, and so was linked to this soul, or inner life, of humanity. So when he died, he died as the representative of the human race to which he belonged.

It is not as though someone other than ourselves

died for us, but we died in him. "One has died for all; therefore all have died" (2 Corinthians 5:14). He "became one with sinful humanity, but without sinning himself. One might compare the water of the Amazon, which becomes the sea, while keeping its waters fresh for many miles out into the ocean through the force of its current.

One might go further and find a link through the energy that sustains the whole universe, and which is in fact the energy of the sustaining power of Christ for "in him all things hold together" (Colossians 1:17). Insofar as the universe has been somehow affected by the fall of man or Satan, Christ was able "to reconcile to himself all things, whether on earth or in heaven, making peace by the blood of his cross" (Colossians 1:20).

The darkening of the sun and the earthquake as Jesus hung on the cross, show the link between his death and the material universe, just as the tearing down of the curtain in the temple which blocked the way into the holy of holies showed that we may now go confidently into the presence of God, "by the new and living way which he opened for us through the curtain, that is, through his flesh" (Matthew 27:51; Hebrews 10:20).

We must not conclude from all this that everyone has been automatically saved. An old saying is that Christ's death is sufficient for all, efficient for some. If salvation is inevitable for all, there would be no need for the New Testament call to personal faith in Jesus Christ.

Note: Prophecy and Prediction

Some years ago, someone invented the slogan, "Prophecy is forthtelling, not foretelling." As so often happens, this either/or idea swept the teaching field, and scholars felt bound to find contemporary applications for everything that the prophets said. But the proper slogan should be, "Prophecy is forthtelling, and sometimes is foretelling."

Jesus Christ told his disciples that there were many prophetic predictions spoken of himself in the Old Testament (Luke 24:25-26,44). Such references are often in the form of preparations for the Messiah, or symbols in parable form of what he came to do, such as in the lay-out of the tabernacle and temple which showed the way to God through sacrifice, and gave aspects of spiritual life in the rules for the sacrifices.

There are also direct prophecies of the coming of the Messiah, and we are familiar with some of them in Stainer's *Crucifixion* and Handel's *Messiah*. It would be strange if nothing was foretold of his death, and indeed Christ himself pinpointed two important prophecies in the Gospels. On the cross, he cried out the opening verse of Psalm 22, "My God, my God, why hast thou forsaken me?" (Matthew 27:46). It is a reasonable supposition that the whole of this psalm ran through his mind while he was on the cross. One has only to read verses 6-21 of Psalm 22 to see the portrayal of the events of which we read in the Gospels.

The other passage is Isaiah 52:13-15, and chapter 53,

beginning with Jesus Christ's battered body, and continuing with the marvel of his death as being for our sins. Both passages conclude with the promise of what he will do after his death, and thus they assume his resurrection.

"I will tell of thy name to my brethren ... All the ends of the earth shall remember and turn to the Lord ..." (Psalm 22:22-27). "When he makes himself an offering for sin, he shall see his offspring, he shall prolong his days ... he shall divide the spoil with the strong; because he poured out his soul to death ..." (Isaiah 53:10-12).

Were David and Isaiah really speaking of Jesus? If David was using powerful metaphors of his own suffering, he must have been guided in his choice of pictures. If Isaiah was writing of the suffering Jewish nation, again he was guided in his choice of fact and theology. Personally I cannot see that either writer was describing anyone other than Jesus Christ.

The prophets rightly believed that God gave them their messages. Since they so often use the term "the Word of the Lord", it is probable that they heard an inner voice conveying words. There were plenty of other claimants to prophetic inspiration, but Jeremiah regards them as victims of what came merely from their own heart, or as we might say, from their own subconscious. They "prophesy the deceit of their own heart ... Who prophesy lying dreams" (Jeremiah 23:25-32).

The people who listened may often have been puzzled as to which prophet was genuine. Generally they followed whoever gave the more congenial message, which left their lives untouched (Jeremiah 23:21-22). Ultimately, proof lay in fulfilment. Thus Jeremiah had a battle with a prophet, Hananiah, and indeed with others also, who said that the exiles in Babylon would shortly be released to come home, whereas God had told Jeremiah that the exile would be long (Jeremiah 28).

The fulfilment of some prophecies had to wait for many years, and we are privileged to have seen them fulfilled. Even the prophets often did not know the exact significance of what God said to them, and 1 Peter 1:10-12, addressed to early Christians, says that the prophets were shown that "they were serving not themselves but you, in the things which have now been announced to you".

> "If I make my bed in Sheol, thou art there!"
>
> *Psalm 139:8*

CHAPTER 9
SIMPLY DEAD

In the Old Testament, *Sheol* is the realm of the departed, corresponding to *Hades* in the New. In contrast to the description of heaven as above, Sheol is thought of as below, the picture language being helped by burial in the earth or in a cave.

One cannot say much about the nature of Sheol, the realm of those who died before the coming of Jesus Christ. Continued existence after death in Old Testament times was negative, and might perhaps be compared to a sort of hibernation. Emphasis is on the handicap of being separated from the body in which one worshipped God and enjoyed the ability to use and increase one's knowledge. The loss of the body consequently brought one into virtual non-existence, (for example Ezekiel 32; Psalm 94:17; Ecclesiastes 9:5). Although the dead are not away from God's presence (Psalm 139:8) they have lost their daily active life in which they knew that God remembered them with his good hand upon them (Psalm 88:5).

Although survival was almost non-existence, there was hope at the end of the tunnel. Thus the psalmist declares, "God will ransom my soul from the power of Sheol, for he will receive me." (Psalm 49:15) and "afterward thou wilt receive me to glory" (Psalm 73:24). One or two passages show that this happy state is connected with resurrection. Thus, Isaiah 26:19 says, "Thy dead shall live, their bodies shall rise. O dwellers in the dust, awake and sing for joy!" Daniel 12:2 declares that "many of those who sleep in the dust of the earth shall awake, some to everlasting life, and some to shame and everlasting contempt". In other words, the loss of the body, which produced the feebleness of Sheol, will one day be made good. One might add the hopes of Job who began by thinking of his death as unending oblivion (Job 14:7-12), and ended with a wish (14:13) and confidence (19:25-37) for resurrection.

There is no need to suppose that the Bible is wrong in all this. The joy that follows our death in Christ could not come before Christ himself came.

Meanwhile, we return to the simple plan of the incarnation. Jesus Christ came to tread the pathway of humanity to the end, and so he died and passed into the existence into which all of us must come – unless we are alive when the Lord returns. His three days without his body formed a brief but real period.

Once or twice I have heard the objection, "Who looked after the world when God died?" The answer is that death is not non-existence. When Jesus told the dying thief, "Truly, I say to you, today you will be with me in Paradise" (Luke 23:43), he was speaking of life, not cessation of life. So we may try to understand, as best we may, what Jesus was doing between the moment of his death on the cross and his resurrection in the garden. But since we are dealing with what was totally unseen, we must rely on such references as there are. Any information must have come from Jesus Christ himself after his resurrection.

When Jesus died on the cross he appeared to his disciples, and to all the world, to be simply dead. One can see the attitude of the disciples by the reaction of the two travellers on the road to Emmaus: intense disappointment and sense of utter failure (Luke 24:19-20).

But appearance was not all. At the moment of dying, Jesus cried out with a loud voice, "Father, into thy hands I commit my spirit" (Luke 23:46). During his lifetime he had committed both body and spirit to his Father to do his will. Now he would do his Father's will in his life in the spirit world. If Sheol or Hades was a state of passivity for ordinary mortals, it must be that Christ's sinlessness and his divine nature enabled him to remain active. Moreover, he was already transforming the old Hades into the new state in which his people will enjoy life in his presence.

So in spirit he passed into the next world. The form of the creed in the Book of Common Prayer says that after death "he descended into hell". This has led some people to say that he went down to Gehenna, the place of eternal separation from God. In fact, "hell" is used in the Authorised (King James) Version of the Bible, and in popular speech, as a translation of Gehenna, the place of ultimate destruction, but it is also used as a translation of Hades or Sheol, the place or state of the departed. The Greek original of the creed says that Jesus Christ descended to Hades, while the Latin version has "he descended to the people below" (descendit ad inferos). There is little doubt that the creeds are simply following through what happens to a human being when he dies. A modern translation has, "He descended to the dead."

We are naturally concerned with the words of Jesus to the dying thief, "Today you shall be with me in paradise." The term *paradise* occurs only twice in the Bible apart from this passage – 2 Corinthians 12:3 and Revelation 2:7. It originally described the magnificent parks or gardens of the Persian kings, but by the time of Christ it was used not only by the Jewish Greek translators of the Old Testament of the garden of Eden, but was also referred by the Jews generally to a happy place after this life, or to heaven itself.

There was no official teaching about its nature or whereabouts, but one may reasonably follow those rabbis who believed it to be what we might call the happy side of Hades. We know that Hades had two divisions, since in his parable of the rich man and Lazarus (Luke 16:19-31) Jesus spoke of the rich man as being in Hades and suffering, while Lazarus was "in Abraham's bosom", which is a symbolic term for a place of honour at the feast (John 13:23). Between the two there was an unbridgeable chasm (Luke 16:26).

It is obvious that Jesus would pass through the gates of death to the happy side of Hades, and he promised that the dying thief would go with him. The intermediate state for us before our resurrection takes on a different quality from what it was before the first coming of Christ, but essentially there will still be a separation of the saved from the lost.

When we ask whether Jesus Christ was doing more than resting during the time when his body was in the tomb, we know that he was active. We are told that he preached, but to whom did he preach and what did he say? The key passage is 1 Peter 3:18-22 and 4:5-6. Here we are told that "in the spirit he went and made his proclamation to the imprisoned spirits. They had refused obedience long ago, while God waited patiently in the days of Noah" (NEB).

What follows may seem rather too technical. If so, please go straight to the closing paragraphs of the chapter.

One interpretation is that Jesus preached the gospel to the Old Testament saints, and thus brought them into the status of Christians saved through his death. This interpretation can be justified by the reference in 1 Peter 4:6 which speaks of the preaching of the gospel to the dead. Also, Ephesians 4:8 speaks of his final ascension to heaven "with captives in his train" (NEB), which may be the Old Testament saints, although later we shall notice a different interpretation.

We must however notice two things here. Although in 1 Peter 4:6 Peter uses the regular word for preaching the gospel, or evangelising, in 3:19 he uses a more general word, "made proclamation". In the next verse the spirits who heard the proclamation are connected with the time of Noah. They are imprisoned, but are not said here to have been the spirits of departed human beings. They are likely to be evil spiritual beings. For Genesis 6:2,4 says that one of the facts which helped to foster the spread of evil was the coming to earth of certain "sons of God" who then had sexual relations with human women. We know from Job 1:6 and 38:7 that the angels were "sons of God", and in Jude 6-7 some of the angels are spoken of as sinning with unnatural lusts like the people of Sodom and Gomorrah.

It has naturally been argued that angels cannot marry, since Christ told the Sadducees that in heaven we shall not marry, but we shall be like the angels (Matthew 22:30). In essence the question that Christ is answering concerns the bearing of children, as the context shows, and the point of Jesus' answer is that the angels do not propagate their race by marriage, since each is a direct creation by God – which of course entitles them to be called "sons of God". Similarly, we become the sons and daughters of God by our direct new creation through the Holy Spirit in response to faith in Christ (John 1:12; Romans 8:15; Galatians 3:26).

If Genesis 6 indicates a fresh fall of angels, we may

assume that this involved materialisation. Appearances of angels in the Old Testament suggest temporary materialisation, since those who appeared to Abraham ate with him, (Genesis 18:1-8), and in Sodom the angels seized Lot and his family by the hand and led them out of the city (Genesis 19:16).

Today the popular mind would be more ready to accept the interpretation we and others have taken of Genesis 6:2 in view of some modern films, where a child is born after intercourse with Satan. One might add that shortly before the time of Christ some Jewish writings, such as the book of Enoch, definitely accepted this interpretation of the fall of angels in Genesis 6:2.

If this is correct, we must interpret the passage in 1 Peter 3:18-22 of Christ's moving from the place of the departed to the place, or sphere, where the fallen spirits (angels) were (Jude 6). He proclaimed his victory to them, to demonstrate that their rebellion against God had come to nothing. Thus the chapter in 1 Peter 3 concludes that Jesus Christ "entered heaven after receiving the submission of angelic authorities and powers" (NEB).

The deliverance of the Old Testament saints is a separate issue. Certainly they were brought through into full remission of their sins through the atoning death of Christ on the cross. In Old Testament times sins were covered, but remained to be brought up and covered again on each Day of Atonement (Hebrews 10:1-4). The covering was by anticipation of the future sacrifice of

Jesus Christ. By analogy one might say that the paper money of the Old Testament was redeemed by the pure gold of the gospel, and thereafter was no longer valid currency.

We should expect that Jesus Christ preached the gospel to these Old Testament believers while he was in Hades, and this is probably the reference in 1 Peter 4:6, where Peter says, "the gospel was preached even to the dead, that though judged in the flesh like men, [that is, they died like all men] they might live in the spirit like God." This is not a mere proclamation as in 3:19, but must refer to the Old Testament believers who were shown that the contents of their faith were fulfilled in Christ. The reference could not be to Christians, since they had been saved in their lifetime.

So after living as man, Jesus Christ passed into the next stage of existence as man, though now incomplete man, since he had left his body in the tomb. We too will pass into a similar state if we die before the Lord returns, as we shall see in the next chapter. The important thing is that now the life in the spirit apart from the body can be an active existence, as it certainly was for Jesus Christ.

Note: The harrowing of hell.
This expression came into use in the Middle Ages. A harrow is used to break up the soil, and Christ was said to have broken up the place of the dead (Hades) and released those whom death and Satan "who has the

power of death" (Hebrews 2:14) held captive. The King of Glory entered in (Psalm 24:7-10), the gates and bars were broken down, and the righteous men of Old Testament times were led out to paradise.

Note 2: Purgatory.
The "official" doctrine of Purgatory is far from happy. A Catholic dictionary defines it as "A place in which souls who depart in the grace of God suffer for a time, because they still need to be cleared from venial (pardonable) sins, or have still to pay the temporal punishment due to mortal (death inflicting) sins, the guilt and punishment of which have been remitted." Thus, purgatory is for Christians, not for unbelievers.

Today more emphasis is laid on our being made fit to endure and enjoy the presence of God. This makes sense, but may not be entirely true. It is not a New Testament concept, since those who are alive when the Lord returns go at once to be "always with the Lord" (1 Thessalonians 4:17). It may be that we have not dared to grasp the power of the precious blood, shed on Calvary, to make us clean from all sin (1 John 1-7). None of us is worthy, but all may be made worthy.

Having said this, there is something to be added. All sin is blotted out in Christ, but we are far from mature in the knowledge of God. In fact we shall never be fully mature, in the sense that the creature can never entirely grasp the being of the Creator. There will always be more to learn and experience of the Trinity all through eternity. Admittedly I cannot quote any text for this, but it is legitimate to say that our whole experience now is growing into God, although God is present with us.

Even though we then see "face to face" and "understand fully" (1 Corinthians 13:12), there will always be room for growth. Indeed, Paul writes these words as analogous to our growth from child to adult. Even an adult is continually learning, although some of his childhood restrictions are removed.

This chapter is concerned with the intermediate state, but growth will be needed when we receive our resurrection bodies. Some object to the introduction of a time element into the intermediate and final state. So far as the intermediate state is concerned, there is a lapse of time between our dying and the Second Coming of Christ when we receive our resurrection bodies. In eternity we can conceive of growth without regarding it in terms of time, although I do not know of anyone who has given a satisfactory picture of eternity and eternal existence.

Up from the grave he arose
  With a mighty triumph o'er his foes.
                                        Robert Lowry

CHAPTER 10
THE RISEN CHRIST

There are many quotations that might have stood at the head of this chapter, but two lines from this hymn emphasise the truth of the resurrection which some theologians tend to bypass today. Resurrection is more than the survival of the spirit. The disciples, as godly Jews, firmly believed in the continued life of Jesus after his death. He had been gathered to his fathers, as Abraham, David and Isaiah had been, and they assumed that this must be the end for the time being.

But now came the amazing resurrection of Jesus. It was first discovered through the tomb being found empty early in the morning. The body of Jesus had gone. Naturally, the disciples were afraid at first that the body had been stolen. But then came the second proof. Jesus Christ appeared to them in bodily form and demonstrated that he was not a spirit or ghost, but that he had a tangible body (Luke 24:36-43). Yet his body was not exactly the same as it had been before. Although it bore the marks of the crucifixion (Luke 24:39; John 20:27), it now had new and transformed qualities. Thus he appeared to his disciples in the room where they were meeting, although the doors were shut (John 20:19,26). He discounted any idea that he was simply a spirit or ghost, since his hands and feet and side still bore the marks of the crucifixion, and he was able to eat in the presence of his disciples (Luke 24:36-43; John 20:24-29).

From this time onwards, the New Testament always speaks of Jesus Christ as risen, and Peter's words on the day of Pentecost make it clear what Christ's resurrection involved. "Nor did his flesh see corruption" (Acts 2:31). Some have maintained that Paul makes no mention of the empty tomb, but only of the spiritually risen Christ. What is not noticed is that the words "resurrection" and "risen from the dead" inevitably mean an empty tomb, for when "resurrection" is used of a dead body it never means less than this. If the tomb had not been empty, the Jews and Christians might have spoken of spiritual survival, but not of resurrection.

Thus when Jesus raised Lazarus from the dead (John 12:9), he came out of the tomb. The difference between him and Jesus is that Lazarus eventually died again, while Jesus, with his newly transformed body, never died a second time.

There is not the slightest doubt that all the Christians in New Testament times believed in the empty tomb as essential for the resurrection of Jesus Christ. At the same time this was more than an historical fact. It formed the ground, first for actual appearances of the Lord, and then for the real sense of union with him. Only in the spiritual sense could the term be used of Christians in this life who were linked to him because he had actually been raised from the dead (Romans 6:4-11; Ephesians 2:6; Colossians 3:1-4).

We must remember that Jesus Christ came into the world to experience what every human being undergoes. Thus he lived, died, and, while his body lay sleeping in the tomb, lived in what we call the intermediate state, as we saw in the previous chapter. This is the destiny which all of us will experience unless we are alive when the Lord returns and our bodies are instantly transformed (1 Thessalonians 4:15-17; Philippians 3:20-21).

Paul speaks of himself sometimes as being alive when the Lord returns (1 Thessalonians 4:15) and sometimes as being among the dead who are raised up (1 Corinthians 6:14; 2 Corinthians 4:14). He did not believe that Jesus was bound to return very soon, but he was ready to meet him when he did appear, as we also should be.

He hoped that he would indeed be alive when Christ returned, so that he would instantly receive his new body, instead of passing first through a state of nakedness without his body, even though he would be in the face-to-face presence with the Lord even without his body (2 Corinthians 5:1-6). The intermediate state is a state of incompleteness, since God did not make man as pure spirit, like the angels, but as spirit plus body. But since spirit can and does survive apart from the body we can, without the body, enjoy the face-to-face presence of Christ, as the angels do.

Since in this book we are following through the events of the incarnation, true God becoming true man, we have tried to see how the steps in his life tally with ours. A difference now arises in that Jesus was able to return to the body in which he had lived, whereas the bodies of Christians down the ages have long since disintegrated. In what way, then, can we follow Christ's footsteps, or how did he follow the way of all mankind? The Bible speaks of resurrection for all mankind, but how are we to understand this?

We have already said that man without a body is not the complete being that God made. Therefore, if death has the last word by killing the body, God and man have been defeated. Yet if the body has been burnt to ashes or dissolved in the grave, how can it be restored? Without falling back on total miracle, yet without trying to make out that we can recreate our bodies without the supernatural hand of God, we must consider how our present bodies are built up. Why do the bodies of even identical twins differ to some extent, while other bodies which seem to have very similar beginnings differ very much indeed?

We hear much about psychosomatic illnesses. This means that an illness or disability seems to be perfectly genuine, but deep investigation may show that the symptoms are caused from the mind. Every one of us recognises that certain facial characteristics show one's character: for example crossness, grumbling, cruelty, happy disposition. Conversion to Jesus Christ is another striking example. The features and behaviour of a person who has a sudden conversion are commonly very different from what they were before, particularly if the previous life has been bad. Missionary photographs of converts before and after conversion illustrate this in a striking way.

Basically this means that an inner attitude of mind helps to build up the body. It is not the food and drink alone that make us as we are, but our mind, soul or spirit takes what is available and produces a body which is *us*.

Cannot a similar thing happen at the resurrection? The resurrection of the dead is always in the New Testament linked to the Second Coming of Christ (1 Corinthians 15:21-23; Philippians 3:20-21; 1 Thessalonians 4:16). Some people object to the introduction of a time element into the intermediate state, and like to think that the resurrection for Christians comes immediately after death. Without saying that in the intermediate bodiless state we experience exactly the same stream of time as we do on earth, we are bound to say that since Jesus Christ has not yet returned as promised, the resurrection of believers has not yet happened.

When the moment comes for the resurrection, my own belief is that once again our spirit will be given the power to build up a body as the expression of itself, but with the new capacities, such as the risen human body of Jesus had (Philippians 3:21).

The wonderful thing will be that we shall fashion our body not only as the recognisable person that we were, but also we shall express Christ in a way in which we could only begin to do during our life on earth. If anything remains of our earthly bodies, we shall presumably draw this into our new bodies, transformed as was the resurrection body of Jesus.

This miracle is possible only through the action of the Holy Spirit. The Bible never says that Jesus Christ raised himself from the dead, nor can we by ourselves create our new resurrection bodies. A key verse is Romans 8:11. "If the Spirit of him who raised Jesus from the dead dwells in you, he who raised Christ Jesus from the dead will give life to your mortal bodies also through his Spirit which dwells in you."

The same work of the Holy Spirit is implied in 2 Corinthians 5:5 where Paul, after speaking of the resurrection of Christians, says, "He who has prepared us for this very thing is God, who has given us the Spirit as a guarantee." Above all, Philippians 3:20-21 says that "the Lord Jesus Christ will change our lowly body to be like his glorious body, by the power which enables him even to subject all things to himself."

But what about those who are not saved in this life? I do not propose here to discuss the state of those who have never heard of the gospel, nor of the future of those who have heard and rejected. I am concerned now only with their resurrection (John 5:29). The difference between them and Christians in the intermediate state is illustrated by the story of Dives, the rich man, in Luke 16:19-31. In the intermediate state (Hades) Dives is in torment, presumably because he has lived only in and for the body, and now he burns with the desires of the body without any body with which to express them.

The Christian on the other hand has the Spirit link with the Lord, so does not miss the body in the same way. When the moment of resurrection comes, the unconverted can merely rebuild his body as the expression of what he was on earth, and still is. He lacks the transforming Holy Spirit.

Some readers will think that I have been too matter-of-fact in describing our resurrection. We cannot know everything, but during much of my life I have been thinking these things out. One day we shall all know, and I am looking forward to the reality when it comes. In our material existence on earth, it is very difficult to describe spiritual existence in words. But it is worth trying, without being irreverent, or without leaving out the face-to-face experience of Father, Son and Holy Spirit, as regrettably some Spiritualists do in their desire for communication with the departed.

Note 1: The Events on the Resurrection Morning
At first sight it is not easy to bring together the accounts of the resurrection morning as they are told in the four

Gospels. Some have given up any attempt at harmonizing, pointing out that when several people give an account of some exciting event, there are bound to be some discrepancies. One can accept that there may be apparent discrepancies, which may turn out to be real differences, but it is always right to see whether they can be harmonised. This is especially important where Bible records are concerned.

It is perfectly possible to make a coherent sense of the accounts of the discovery of the empty tomb, and it would be even easier if we had been told the exact whereabouts of the participants before and after the visit to the tomb. As it is, we can make reasonable suggestions.

Where did the disciples and the women spend the next two nights after the crucifixion? One thinks of them as staying in Jerusalem, but it is more likely that some returned to Bethany where they had stayed with Jesus during the previous nights. John was an exception, since he must have had a house in Jerusalem to which he took Mary the mother of Jesus from the tragic scene at the cross. "From that hour the disciple (John) took her to his own home" (John 19:27). Later he was joined by Peter, since John and Peter were together when the news came of Jesus' resurrection (John 20:2).

Matthew, Mark and Luke relate the coming of the women to the tomb. If we assume that they came from Bethany, the two mile walk would be easy. All three Synoptic Gospels name two of them as Mary Magdalene and Mary the mother of James, who was probably James the son of Alphaeus (Matthew 10:3). Mark adds Salome. There is some reason for identifying Salome with the mother of James and John. Luke adds the name of Joanna, who was the wife of Herod's steward (Luke 8:3), but says that there were other women also (23:55 and 24:10).

While we have suggested that the women came from Bethany, it is likely that Joanna, as the wife of Herod's steward, would have spent the two nights in Jerusalem, and one or two of the women may have lodged with her. This is an example of the help it would be if we had more details.

So a party of women came to the tomb at first light. It has been suggested that in the semi-darkness they went to the wrong tomb, which was empty, and mistakenly thought it was the tomb in which Jesus had been buried. The absurdity of this suggestion becomes obvious if we ask ourselves what would happen if we heard that some well-known leader had emerged from his grave, and left it gapingly empty.

Any number of people would hurry out to the cemetery to check for themselves. So if the women had mistaken the tomb in the darkness, there would have been plenty who would soon have discovered the actual tomb for themselves when it was day.

Mary Magdalene was the first to react. She, and the others who had been discussing who would roll back the heavy stone for them, noticed as they approached that the stone had been rolled back. They assumed the worst, after the troubles that there had been with the Jews, and Mary Magdalene ran full tilt to John's house to say that the body must have been removed from the tomb by persons unknown, and taken elsewhere (John 20:1-2).

When we read what follows in John 20, it is impossible not to see it as the description of an eyewitness, John, whereas the other Gospels are dependent on what they heard from those who had taken part. The story tells how John and Peter ran to the tomb to see for themselves. John stooped to look into the tomb, and saw that it was empty, except for the linen cloths that had been wrapped round the body. The more impulsive Peter went into the tomb, and presumably John followed. They saw the linen cloths on the stone slab, and the head cloth lying separately, showing that the body had risen through the shrouds, and had not been carried away.

But meanwhile the other women had gone, finding the whole situation too frightening. Matthew says that an angel had already rolled back the stone before the women arrived. The angel may not have remained outside, since otherwise Mary Magdalene would have seen him as she approached. Mark says that the women entered the tomb and there saw a young man in white. This would be the angel who had rolled back the stone, but no longer appearing frightening as he had appeared to the guards (Matthew 28:3).

The angel announced that Jesus had risen, and commissioned the women to tell his disciples and Peter that they should return to Galilee, where they would see him as of old.

Luke says that the women went into the tomb and found two men in dazzling raiment, angels, who reminded them that Jesus had told the disciples that he would rise from the dead on the third day. They remembered this, and went and told the apostles what they had seen and heard. It is possible that some saw one angel and others two, since spirit beings may be present without being seen by everyone. For example, Balaam could not see an angel until the Lord opened his eyes (Numbers 22:31).

Others think that there were two groups of women who came independently to the tomb, and we have already seen that they may have come from Bethany and Jerusalem. One group found one angel, and the other two. Certainly Luke writes rather strangely in 24:10, although some modern translations, such as the RSV, disguise this. What he actually says in the Greek is: "There were Mary Magdalene and Joanna and Mary the mother of James," – one sentence with a main verb. He continues with another sentence with a verb. "And the other women [or, the other women also] together with them told these things to the apostles." So Luke may indicate that the named women had the experience that Matthew and Mark record, but the unnamed women from Galilee (Luke 23:55), referred to as "they" in 24:1, had the further experience that he records.

Mark says that the women were too frightened to tell anyone. Matthew says that as they ran to tell the disciples, Jesus met them, and as they worshipped him he gave them a similar message to that which the angel had given, at the same time telling them not to be afraid.

We can bring the accounts in Matthew and Mark together by our assumption that these women had come from Bethany and were now running to give the news to the disciples there. They were too afraid to find John and Peter in Jerusalem, where they might well be in danger from supporters of the priests. But some certainly returned after meeting Jesus and took their news to the disciples (Luke 24:10).

Meanwhile we return to Mary Magdalene. She could not keep pace with John and Peter, and they had run back with their news before she arrived. She looked into the tomb and saw two angels sitting at either end where the body of Jesus had been. She spoke to them, and then turned round and saw a man whom she took to be the gardener, and who she thought might have taken the body away. The story of how the man showed himself to be Jesus is one of the most touching in the Bible.

He told Mary not to cling to him, but to tell his brethren that the next significant step in his time on earth would be his return to his Father. It is quite possible that "my brethren" in John 20:17 means the members of Jesus' family and not the disciples. *Every* occurrence of "his brethren" in this Gospel is a reference to Jesus' brothers (John 2:12; 7:3,5,10), except the reference to his disciples as "brethren" in 21:23.

Since Mary Magdalene was the first to see the Risen Lord, if we can trust the tradition in the so-called "lost end of Mark" (Mark 16:9) – and there is no reason to doubt it in the light of the record in John's Gospel – the appearance of Jesus to her took place before the appearance to the women on the way to Bethany.

When Paul records the resurrection and subsequent appearances in 1 Corinthians 15:1-9, he names Peter (Cephas) as one who saw Jesus before his appearance to the Twelve in the evening, and to more than five hundred at once, perhaps in Galilee. Jesus also appeared to his brother James. Peter is mentioned as the leader after Pentecost, and James, the Lord's brother, became the head of the church in Jerusalem. We should love to have an account of the conversations between Peter who had denied Jesus, and Jesus' brother who had previously not believed in him as the Messiah (John 7:3-5).

Then Paul names himself as having had a face-to-face meeting with the Lord on the Damascus road. So the three commissioned leaders each had their call from the risen Lord. It is curious that Paul twice mentions an appearance to the twelve disciples (1 Corinthians 15:5,7). Perhaps Luke, his travelling companion, had told him of the appearance in the upper room in the evening (Luke 24:36), and had also described the coming together of the apostles on the Mount of Olives to witness Christ's ascension (Acts 1:6-12).

Note 2: The Three Days

The Jews, and some others, did not count as we do, but reckoned a part of a day as a whole in numbering. The Jewish day ran from sunset to sunset. Thus, when Jesus died on the cross at 3 p.m., the period 3 p.m. to sunset was *day one*. Friday sunset to Saturday sunset was *day two*, and *day three* began at Saturday sunset, so that Jesus rose on *day three* (Sunday). We have no right to alter this standard method of reckoning and try to date the crucifixion on Thursday, as some have done.

An excellent and full treatment of the resurrection stories is *Easter Enigma*, by John Wenham (Paternoster Press, 1984). The book was published after I had written this chapter.

> Jesus reigns, adored by angels;
> Man with God is on the throne.
>> *Hymn: See, the Conqueror mounts in triumph*

CHAPTER 11
THE ASCENSION TO THE RIGHT HAND OF THE FATHER

In writing of the earthly life, death and resurrection of the Lord Jesus Christ, we have been able to work on a basis of historical fact. With the ascension we begin with a fact of history, but then pass into an unseen phase which is at the root of Christian experience, but which can with difficulty be expressed in words.

The historical fact can be taken first. The careful historian, Luke, who in his travels with Paul must have met most of the apostles, has recorded their story of the ascension in Acts 1 and Luke 24:50-53.

For forty days after his resurrection, Jesus had appeared repeatedly to his disciples, and had taught them the significance of the Old Testament Scriptures and what was to be the content of their Christian preaching (Luke 24:45-49; Acts 1:1-3). Now he led them to Bethany on the further side of the Mount of Olives, and after telling them to wait in Jerusalem until the coming of the Holy Spirit upon them, "he was lifted up, and a cloud took him out of their sight".

The disciples stared upwards, until two angels in appearance like men clothed in white told them that although Jesus had been taken into heaven he would one day return in the same way as they had seen him go.

In Chapter 2 we discussed the matter of heaven above, and noticed that the word *above* had the significance of *away from* the earth, so that from any spot in the world, heaven, where God is served absolutely and freely, is *above*. The Lord's Prayer is meaningless unless this is so. "Thy will be done on earth, as it is in heaven."

Thus Christ's ascension was largely an acted parable to show that his time on earth was over, and his followers must not expect him to return to earth again until his Second Coming. So we can still regard the ascension as included in the simplicity of the incarnation.

But when we ask what actually happened after the cloud received him, we can go only a limited way. Indeed, we are not required to go further than to dwell on genuine Christian experience, as we find in the New Testament the *effects* of the ascension to the right hand of the Father.

The Holy Spirit interprets these effects to us. That is why Jesus told the disciples to wait in Jerusalem for the coming of the Holy Spirit. When he came at Pentecost, the Christians immediately began to preach the claims of Jesus Christ. The Holy Spirit did not come as another incarnation, but as the channel through which Jesus

Christ could be received in the central control point of men, women and children. "Through him [Jesus Christ] we have access in [or by] one Spirit to the Father" (Ephesians 2:18). This is the Trinity in operation.

The Spirit helps us to understand the nature of the atonement, and ultimately draws us to accept Christ as our Saviour. Thereafter he makes the spiritual presence of Christ real, both with us and especially in us. So although Christ is in heaven, he is here on earth through the Holy Spirit. The two come together in Romans 8:9-10, "You are not in the flesh, you are in the Spirit, if in fact the Spirit of God really dwells in you. Any one who does not have the Spirit of Christ does not belong to him. But if Christ is in you ..."

I am not trying to minimise the direct work of the Holy Spirit, since many charismatics have found tremendous release through opening up to the Holy Spirit. A personal note may be in place. When I was at Cambridge a small group of us converted Christians rather set ourselves up as "knowing the Holy Spirit". Before the days of charismatic experiences in the churches and Christian unions, we did all in our power to have full experiences of the Spirit. It was almost as though we were treating the Holy Spirit as extra to Jesus Christ.

In the end I returned to what I believe to be a truer belief. The fullness of the Spirit means a fuller experience of Jesus Christ, but over-concentration on the working of the Spirit may mean a diminution of the experience of Jesus Christ, even though the result is stimulating experiences.

So far we have thought of individual Christian experience, and this is the foundation of "Evangelicalism" – if we may use traditional terminology. "Catholicism" (not only Roman Catholicism) has a different approach by way of the church. To make a distinction, it has been said, "Evangelicals believe that one becomes a Christian through faith in Jesus Christ, while Catholics believe that one becomes a member of Christ through becoming a member of the church." As an evangelical, brought up as an Anglo-Catholic, I can see the tension. This tension at the present time is seen especially in the search for church unity.

Evangelicals do not trouble so much about tidying up denominational relationships. I personally find little difficulty in accepting other ministries and, at the grassroots, Christians of various denominations are happy to meet together without waiting for councils and synods to draw up minimum terms of agreement. Our main concern is the reality of Christian faith.

If a person has a genuine love for Christ, I am happy to worship and to receive the sacrament with him. If his beliefs about Jesus Christ differ slightly from mine, I may discuss but not argue. But if his views are derogatory to Jesus as the New Testament presents him, I find it hard to have fellowship with him except on a social level.

It has been good to see that there has been fresh

fellowship between Catholics and Evangelicals in recent years. This has become possible on the basis of the Bible and real inner experience. But we still are aware of the distinction that we made above. The Catholic is naturally concerned with the true church, with traditions which have grown up on the basis of texts in the New Testament. An example is the "Thou art Peter" statement for Roman Catholics.

We cannot here spend time in discussing individual points, but the most important things for formal agreement are the validity of the sacraments and the authority of the ministers. To the Catholic these are essential marks of the true church, plus of course true doctrine.

We come back to the balance between individualism and the church. The ascension and its effects are seen in the church, since the Holy Spirit has come to be the life of the church, and thus to make the life of Christ effective in the church. In fact Ephesians shows that the church is the body of Christ, and Christ is the head "from whom the whole body, joined and knit together by every joint with which it is supplied, when each part is working properly, makes bodily growth and upbuilds itself in love" (Ephesians 4:15-16).

The Catholic asks himself, Do I belong to the true church, the one body of Christ on earth? (Ephesians 4:4). The evangelical says, Do I belong to Christ? If so, I am bound to be a member of the true church, his one body.

The reference to the ascension in Ephesians 4:8-12 inclines to the corporate side. Here Paul quotes Psalm 68:18, which celebrates the victory of God as he "ascends the high mount" with captives in his train. The words are well applied to Jesus Christ as he returns to heaven. We saw in an earlier chapter that the captives may be Old Testament prisoners released from Satan's hold. But they may also be the principalities and powers of evil, who were triumphed over on the cross, as is stated in Colossians 2:15.

Paul changes the quotation slightly when he substitutes "Gave gifts to men" for the psalmist's "received gifts among men" (NEB). This is a justifiable alteration, since a conqueror commonly distributed a large part of the spoils to his supporters. Similarly, Paul shows that Christ gave to his church the gift of ministers to build up the people of God, so that they too can take up the task of building up the body.

Thus the emphasis here is not on the individual so much as on the welfare of the corporate body. Similarly in 1 Corinthians 12:12-30 the gifts from the Holy Spirit are given to individuals, including leaders, but all are for the well-being of the body of Christ, the church.

So the New Testament finds room for the individual to approach the risen Christ directly, and for the church to incorporate the individual in the body of Christ on earth. Those today who react against the masculinity of the Deity, may note that the church is spoken of as feminine, and as the bride of Christ (Ephesians 5:28-32;

Revelation 19:7-8; 21:2). We need more than one picture to reveal heavenly relationships, and there is room to stress both the individual and the corporate church.

There are other pictures of the ascended state. Christ is seated at the right hand of the Father. The most frequently quoted Old Testament verse in the New Testament is Psalm 110:1. "Sit at my right hand, till I make your enemies your footstool." Jesus Christ is now at the place of all rule and power, but there are still enemies to be conquered, as well we know. One of the last words of Jesus Christ on earth was, "All authority in heaven and on earth has been given to me. Go therefore and make disciples of all nations" (Matthew 28:18-19). The wars of conquest and defence, begun against earthly enemies in Old Testament times, are to be completed now against the ultimate enemies of God and his people, sin and Satan (Ephesians 6:10-18).

The other picture of the ascended state is of Christ as the eternal priest. This is the theme of the epistle to the Hebrews. The Catholic interpretation is that Christ is eternally offering himself in heaven, and gives himself to be offered, not sacrificed, on earth in the consecrated bread and wine in the Eucharist. I have mentioned differences between Evangelical and Catholic interpretations in this book. Catholic readers will know what they hold. As an evangelical, I am bound to say why I differ on this point.

We agree that Jesus Christ superseded the old priesthood when he offered the sacrifice of himself on the cross, and by virtue of this sacrifice he broke down the barrier, represented by the veil in the temple, so that the way into the holy of holies in which God manifested his presence is now open (Hebrews 9:1-10; 10:1-22). He has become our priest through whom we approach God.

Where we differ is over the present functions of Jesus Christ as priest. Must a priest be continually offering? Many of us say No, any more than a woman must be continually bearing children in order to be a mother.

One baby makes her a mother, and one offering makes Christ a priest. The English translation in the KJV and RSV of Hebrews 8:3 has inadvertently suggested that Jesus Christ, as priest, must continue to offer. "It is necessary for this priest also to have something to offer." In the Greek there is no verb ("is") with "necessary", as the KJV italics show. Hence the NEB margin supplies the past instead of the present "must have had," and this fits the theme of Hebrews.

The whole force of the argument in Hebrews 7:21 to 10:25 is on the once and for all sacrificial work of Christ. In particular, Hebrews 10:12 seems conclusive. "When Christ had offered for all time a single sacrifice for sins, he sat down at the right hand of God." The seated Christ is contrasted with the standing priest who offers sacrifices repeatedly (verse 11).

But his intercession for us is repeated; "... who is at the right hand of God, who indeed intercedes for us" (Romans 8:54). "He is able for all time to save those who draw near to God through him, since he always lives to make intercession for them" (Hebrews 7:25). The Catholic naturally links this to the belief that Jesus Christ is continually pleading his sacrifice in heaven.

I have always found these two verses difficult in the light of Christ's own words in John 16:26-27: "In that day you will ask in my name; and I do not say to you that I shall pray the Father for you; for the Father himself loves you." What is certain is that we cannot treat Jesus as being more loving than the Father, and ask him to persuade the Father to grant what otherwise he would be unwilling to give.

However we understand Christ's intercession, we can agree on one thing: his presence on the throne in his risen life after his sacrificial death is in itself an intercession for us, as perhaps Hebrews 7:25 indicates.

What really matters is not full agreement on how Christ represents us in heaven, but the enjoyment of being in the immediate presence of God through being in him. The Holy Spirit not only is the vehicle of Christ in the individual and the church on earth, but he links us to Christ in heaven (Ephesians 2:6; Hebrews 10:19-22). When we kneel or sit beside fellow Christians at the Lord's Supper or Holy Communion, we must accept him or her without examining them to see whether their belief about the sacrament is exactly the same as ours.

I have left until last a question to which I do not know the answer. To those readers who feel that I have professed to explain everything, it will come as a relief to discover that there is something I do not know! I am not aware of any orthodox theologian who has answered the question, or even asked it, so perhaps it is foolish to ask. But for completeness we ought to ask it, although we must remember the words of Deuteronomy 29:29, "The secret things belong to the LORD our God; but the things that are revealed belong to us and to our children for ever, that we may do all the words of this law."

Up until now we have thought of things that God has revealed which will enable us better to live the Christian life. The answer to my question has not in any way been revealed at all.

The question is this: Where at the present moment is the risen body of Jesus Christ? We have noticed some of the properties of this body in the period between the resurrection and the ascension. It was evidently in one place at one time, though able to remain invisible. I refer to the presence of the actual body, and not to any extended spiritual presence.

We saw earlier in the book that some devout Christians are unable to think of heaven in any other than material terms. If this were true, heaven would be somewhere in the galaxy, and there would be no difficulty in locating Christ's body there. The Mormons in fact believe that God has a body, and that there is a star or planet called Kolob, "which is set nigh unto the throne of God" (*Pearl of Great Price. Abraham 3*).

The modern Aetherius Society has had a revelation that the Master Jesus apparently lives on or near Venus.

I personally believe that the Bible is less materialistic in speaking of heaven, but I think that those who picture a throne on a heavenly planet are nearer the truth than those who depersonalise God and dissolve Jesus Christ into spirit alone.

Although theologians have written little or nothing about the ascended body of Jesus Christ, they have certainly held that he has retained his human nature, and because of the inner link that binds humanity together we can say that we have been taken up in him. Another picture is that he is our representative on the throne of God. Perhaps this is simpler, since he is sinless, while we are sinful and consequently find it difficult to regard ourselves as linked to him in heaven. He represents us insofar as he and we are members of the human race, but we are in him in a special way as redeemed and cleansed members of humanity. Vital union with the risen Christ is described in Ephesians 2:4-6: "But God, who is rich in mercy, out of the great love with which he loved us, even when we were dead through our trespasses, made us alive together with Christ (by grace you have been saved), and raised us up with him, and made us sit with him in the heavenly places in Christ Jesus."

But where is the body? It cannot have been dissolved, since we know that Jesus will come in the same way as he was seen to go into heaven, as the disciples were told when they saw his body ascend (Acts 1:11). Jesus himself said that all will see him coming on the clouds of heaven (Matthew 24:30). This implies the return of his body.

We can only say that however good we may be as visualisers or intellectual calculators, we can neither visualise heaven nor work out its nature. Perhaps CS Lewis said all that can be said: "Jesus apparently passed into some spatial relationship with a new universe" (Minutes of a talk in Oxford, quoted in *CS Lewis at the Breakfast Table* Macmillan, 1979, p.151).

Meanwhile we experience his presence with us and in us, beamed in by the Holy Spirit, nonetheless real, although his natural body is absent. This is where we shall differ from him when we have received our resurrection bodies. We shall not be everywhere, as he, the God-Man, is.

What is man? ... thou dost crown him with glory and honour. Thou hast given him dominion over the works of thy hands; thou hast put all things under his feet.

Psalm 8:4-6

CHAPTER 12
THE RULE OF GOD, THE RULE OF MAN

We have already spoken of the coming of the Holy Spirit at Pentecost, and his mediation of the presence of Christ. Yet this was not the Second Coming of which Christ spoke, since after Pentecost the writers of the New Testament were still looking for Christ to come again. Indeed, at every service of the Holy Communion, the Lord's Supper, or the Eucharist, (whatever title we use) we "proclaim the Lord's death until he comes" (1 Corinthians 11:26).

There are varying attempts to describe how Jesus Christ will return, and what he will do when he comes, but we must try to concentrate on the basic facts.

He will be seen returning to this earth from above. This was the promise of the angels at the ascension (Acts 1:11). Paul speaks of his descent from heaven (1 Thessalonians 4:16). Christ himself said, "they will see the Son of man coming in clouds with great power and glory" (Mark 13:26). Peter speaks of the chief Shepherd being manifested (1 Peter 5:4) and of the revealing of Jesus Christ (1:7). John says that "when he appears we shall be like him, for we shall see him as he is" (1 John 3:2).

We may sum up with Paul's words in Philippians 3:20-21: "Our commonwealth is in heaven, and from it we await a Saviour, the Lord Jesus Christ, who will change our lowly body to be like his glorious body, by the power which enables him even to subject all things to himself."

It may sound naive to take the Second Coming texts literally and look for Jesus Christ's appearance from the sky, but it is no more unscientific or unnatural to believe this than it would have been in 100 BC to believe that God would be born as a baby from a virgin mother. The birth occurred as a fact of history, and the descent from heaven will equally be a fact.

We are told, "Behold, he is coming with the clouds, and every eye will see him" (Revelation 1:7). Some have recently interpreted this statement as meaning that he will be seen on television, but it seems to me that the artificial satellites offer a more sensible clue. Some satellites can be seen in all parts of the world as the earth rotates. If Jesus Christ descended visibly to the earth over a period of twenty-four hours or more from a great height, he could be seen by "every eye".

I know that some will think that this is far too literal an interpretation, but I would ask them to suggest an alternative. Why should we be agnostic when the Bible gives us a consistent picture? I take the interpretation of Matthew 24:30 that the appearance of "the sign of the Son of man in heaven" is the promised Son of man, Christ himself.

The people of God will be associated with Jesus in his return. If we examine Paul's words in 1 Thessalonians 4:14-18, we find that through Jesus, God will bring back with Jesus those who though they have fallen asleep, still live, and they will receive their new bodies as Christians, followed in turn by living Christians. Paul is saying what is said by the much maligned hymn,

> On the resurrection morning
> Soul and body meet again.

The souls or spirits of the departed return with Christ, and then receive their resurrection bodies. Christians who are still alive will at the same time have their natural bodies changed to spiritual (Philippians 3:20-21; 2 Corinthians 5:2-4).

Here we must take sides over standard interpretations. First, over the time of the rapture – which is the technical term for the catching up of the people of God to meet the Lord. On the basis of certain periods mentioned in Daniel and Revelation, some have concluded that the rapture will occur seven years before the visible appearing of Christ, after which there will be a period of great tribulation which will include the appearance of a Satanically inspired figure, known as the Antichrist.

It is thought that the church will escape this terrible time. Others believe that the church will go through this tribulation. Yet again others, among whom I include myself, believe that the great tribulation denotes the persecutions and false teachings down the ages. We expect to see an intensification of these attacks before the Lord comes. Thus we in the West have been attacked by devious teachings, while in some other countries there has been an outburst of anti-God persecution. At the same time we have been encouraged by signs of revival, return to the truth, and faithfulness under persecution.

The second point of difference concerns the Millennium, that is, the reign of Christ on earth for a thousand years. The only detailed description of it that the Bible gives is in Revelation 20:1-6. Here it is said than an angel binds Satan in the bottomless pit and seals it over him, so that he should deceive the nations no more for a thousand years.

The passage goes on to speak of those who reign with Christ. Specially mentioned are those who gave their lives for testifying to Jesus Christ, and those who, whether or not they were martyred, had refused to worship the false standards presented by Satan, and had refused to belong to him.

Meanwhile those who died without Christ wait for their resurrection and assessment until the end of the thousand years. Those who are raised will never die again, but rule as Christ's representatives.

What is the meaning of all this? When I was a young Christian the universal interpretation among evangelicals was that after his coming, Jesus Christ would reign on earth for a thousand years. Many associated this reign with the conversion of the Jews who would enjoy the literal experience of the national promises in the Old Testament.

Then a leading evangelical wrote a book which gave arguments for treating the *whole* of the Christian era as being the Millennium, and a number of evangelical scholars agreed. It can be argued that the book of Revelation falls into seven sections, of which the first six each take up some aspect of the trials of the church down the ages. Must not the seventh section have a similar interpretation? I personally have found that the Revelation has become a new book since it was pointed out to me that most of it presents pictures of the whole Christian era rather than a comparatively short period at the time of the end. But I still believe that the final section (Revelation 19:11 to 22:19) is a winding up description, leading to the eternal bliss of heaven.

A comparison of two passages in the book leads to this conclusion beyond any reasonable doubt. In Revelation 12:7-12 we have the picture of Satan cast down to the earth. The result is woe for the earth, and woe for the people of God, described in greater detail in the following chapter. This describes Satan's active work on earth since Calvary. In 20:1-3 Satan is bound, and sealed in the bottomless pit for a thousand years so that he can deceive the nations no more.

These two pictures in the same book are diametrically opposed, and cannot in my opinion refer to the same event. Everywhere else in the book, and in the New Testament in general, Satan is spoken of as a conquered but still active foe on earth. He is not imprisoned in the bottomless pit, although some of his angels are already there (2 Peter 2:4; Jude 6).

Readers will realise that these are differing views, but it makes sense to interpret the Millennium as being a period of Christ's reign on earth. We need not insist on exactly a thousand years, since in this book numbers are commonly used symbolically.

Does such a millennial reign on earth fit in with what I have called the Simplicity of the Incarnation? Is Christ's reign to be limited to his spiritual rule from heaven? Certainly the two types of reign are not contradictory. Since the Bible does not explain the reason for a millennial reign on earth, one can only speculate about it, and readers must realise that as with some other things in this book, my suggestions are ideas that others must weigh up.

In Genesis 1:26-28 God gave men and women dominion over the world, presumably to act as God's representatives. This is taken up in Psalm 8:6-8, "Thou hast given him dominion over the works of thy hands; thou hast put all things under his feet." This psalm is quoted in Hebrews 2:6-9 with the comment, "Now in putting everything in subjection to him, he left nothing outside his control. As it is, we do not yet see everything in subjection to him. But we see Jesus, who for a little while was made lower than the angels, crowned with glory and honour because of the suffering of death, so that by the grace of God he might taste death for every one." In the following verse Jesus is spoken of as "he for whom and by whom all things exist", which reminds us of Colossians 1:16, "All things were created through him and for him." Jesus is the fulfilment of God's purpose for man.

Yet of Jesus, as of man in general, we can use the words of Hebrews 2:8. "We do not yet see everything in subjection to him." The ascension promise, based on Psalm 110, is that Jesus Christ is to sit at the Father's right hand until his enemies are made his footstool. So enemies still remain.

We commonly assume that all these promises belong to eternity, as indeed they will finally be fulfilled then. But surely there is some need for them to be fulfilled on earth, so that before the end of all things, man, that is the incarnate Man, will exercise dominion as God originally intended. Otherwise we could plead that it was out of the question for anyone to rule properly and fairly, since we are continually thwarted by sin.

It is impossible to visualise the reign of Jesus Christ on earth. We must assume that it will be a union of perfect love and discipline. Christ's people will be associated with him, as the angels are associated with God at the present time (Revelation 20:4). They will have already received their resurrection bodies. If as seems reasonable there is an earthly centre of government, one would expect this to be Jerusalem, in view of the position given to this city in the Old Testament, and especially in Zechariah 14 which speaks of the coming of the Lord, although there is much that needs sorting out in this and other chapters.

The rest of the world who are alive at the Second Coming will be Christ's willing, or unwilling, subjects. Although Satan is bound, inner sin still remains, and Jesus Christ will show how this can be controlled in the interest of all mankind. The Old Testament ideals, towards which we struggle now, will obviously become realities. Wars will cease (Isaiah 2:4), and various forms of natural power will be safely available for the purposes for which God intended it. There will be proper plans so that all nations can have sufficient for their needs and their enjoyment, and this will mean an end to exploitation by human greed and selfishness (Psalm 145:15-16). Conservation will be a top priority (Psalm 65:9-13; 104:14-16; Isaiah 35:1-2; 41:17-20). One might continue, but the primary fact is that all this displays the character of the Son of David himself, as it is described in Isaiah 11:1-5.

One may assume that people will be shown that what needs to be done, or done away, is for the welfare of all mankind. If it is not done willingly, it must be enforced for the good of the whole. There is a summary in Isaiah 65:21-22 which says, "They shall build houses and inhabit them; they shall plant vineyards and eat their fruit. They shall not build and another inhabit; they shall not plant and another eat." Whatever may have been the first application of these words, they are certainly true of the Millennium.

One would think that a thousand years of Christ's direct rule would mean the conversion of everyone in the world. The suggestion in Isaiah 65:20 is that long life will be normal, even though sinners remain and death will still occur. Perhaps medical science will be augmented under God's guidance. Obviously very many will be converted to Jesus as Saviour, but strangely enough many will not. One meets thinking Christians who hold that ultimately every single person will be saved through their face-to-face contact with God in the next life. But if my interpretation of the Millennium is true, even the close contact with God will leave some unaffected.

So we read in Revelation 20:7-10 that Satan is freed at the end of the thousand years. He entices mankind, as he enticed Eve and Adam, and many follow him in a final revolt against Christ and his people. Satan and all with him are destroyed.

I have not mentioned the place of the Jews in the Millennium. Many Bible students believe that they will be converted to Christ, and be the main agents after the church has been taken away seven years before the Lord's return. If one does not find evidence for this earlier rapture of the church, it is still reasonable to include a number of converted Jews as world evangelists.

Evangelists will be needed to interpret Christ to the nations. A mass conversion of Jews would be a fulfilment of Romans 11:15:26, "So all Israel will be saved," although it is equally possible that this sentence is not exclusive to Judaism, but may emphasise that the true Israel of God needs both Jews and Gentiles for its completion.

We wonder what will happen to the earth after the Millennium. There are two clues. One is in 2 Peter 3:10: "The heavens will pass away with a loud noise, and the elements will be dissolved with fire, and the earth and the works that are upon it will be burned up." The words have been interpreted by some as nuclear destruction. In verse 13, Peter adds, "But according to his promise we wait for new heavens and a new earth in which righteousness dwells."

The other reference is in Revelation 21:1, when John sees, "a new heaven and a new earth; for the first heaven and the first earth had passed away, and the sea was no more". It seems that there will be a purging and rebirth of the present created order, but we are not told whether we shall live in the new earth, or whether we shall live in the sphere of heaven, or even in both.

I am afraid I shall lose some friends over what I have written about the Second Coming and the Millennium. We have already noted disagreements over the time and manner of the coming and the nature of the Millennium. Others will regard me as far too naive. To them I would say, What alternative do you suggest? Some, who have made detailed maps of the future, will think my outline is far too skimpy, and indeed wrong. One day we shall know, and if I am wrong I know that there will be something infinitely better. But there is no harm in trying to look ahead on the basis of what has been revealed.

We have not yet reached the simple climax of the incarnation. At the end of the reign on earth something wonderful happens, which is indeed the divine climax. Paul describes it in 1 Corinthians 15:24-28, "Then comes the end, when he delivers the kingdom to God the Father after destroying every rule and every authority and power ... When all things are subjected to him, then the Son himself will also be subjected to him who put all things under him, that God may be everything to every one."

This is very far from teaching the inferiority of the Son. Rather it sums up the whole thought of the Bible. Jesus Christ does not succumb to the very human wish to set up a private kingdom of his own. He has deserved to be the Lord and King of those whom he has saved at such tremendous cost. But we go back to the story of Eden, where mankind slipped away from God's kingdom in order to be master of his own realm. Might not Jesus Christ have looked on the world and its people, and said, "These are mine"? Instead of that, he offered back to his

Father, God's world, fallen, redeemed, cleansed and renewed, and since this world is now inextricably alive in him, he offers himself.

The world is nothing without himself, and his final purpose is incomplete without the church in which he has expressed himself. And now God is all in all, Father, Son and Holy Spirit. There is no rival kingdom in heaven.

Note: Judgment

There are several aspects of judgment.

1. The primary judgment is passed in Christ. In another sense, it is deliverance *from* judgment, so that a Christian may know that in Christ he will not come into judgment, but has passed from death to life (John 5:24).

2. But for the Christian there is an assessment of what he has done since his conversion. Thus Paul says in 1 Corinthians 3:10-15 that Christ is the only saving foundation, but there will be an assessment of what has been built on the foundation. If the building comes through the test, the Christian will be rewarded. If it fails the test, the owner will indeed be saved, but it will be as though much of his life has been burnt up. Again we are told that "we must all appear before the judgment seat of Christ, so that each one may receive good or evil, according to what he has done in his body" (2 Corinthians 5:10).

It would seem that this assessment gives an indication of the sphere of service in eternity. Thus Christ in one of his parables spoke of the servants who are given responsibilities according to their use of the pounds which the master gave them (Luke 19:12-27).

So for Christians there is salvation through faith in Christ, but an assessment of what has been done on earth. The rewards are not medals, but service.

3) There is another judgment linked to the coming of Christ, commonly spoken of as the Judgment of the Sheep and the Goats (Matthew 25:31-46). The separation between them is on the ground of their unconscious treatment of Christ in the suffering and the deprived. We need not press "my brethren" (verse 40) so as to limit the sufferers to Christians.

The parable teaches salvation through good works without mentioning faith, and to many of us this is a difficulty in view of the New Testament teaching on saving faith. But it does not teach that salvation is deliberately earned. The whole point is that those who go into eternal life are amazed at the significance of the good deeds that they did out of the promptings of their hearts. It may be that here we are given a hint of God's treatment of those who have had no knowledge of Christ in his life. It was the unknown Christ whom they served, or ignored, in sufferers around them.

4). Whether or not we accept my interpretation of the Millennium, there is no doubt that there is a last judgment, described in Revelation 20:11-15. It is the judgment of the Great White Throne. The dead are judged by the books of records of what they did during their lifetime. There is another book opened described as the book of life, which is also called "the Lamb's book of life" in 21:27.

One might suggest that the first books are the consciences of the departed, corresponding to some extent with the experiences of drowning people who see their life passing before them in a few moments of time. Under hypnotism many have been taken back to long-forgotten memories, which shows that somewhere all our experiences are stored and capable of recall, as from a book. Judgment will thus be instantaneous and simultaneous for all. We do not stand waiting in a queue for the verdict from an external book of records.

The book of life is over and above the book of conscience. It must be the same book as Jesus referred to when he said to his disciples, "Rejoice that your names are written in heaven" (Luke 10:20). If the judgment of the Great White Throne comes after the Millennium, this is the judgment of those who were not already saved as Christians at the time of the Lord's return. We are told that there are to be two resurrections, the first of Christians at the Lord's return, the second of the rest of the departed (Revelation 20:5-6).

But this judgment of the Throne includes both saved and lost, which shows that some who were not raised as Christians will now be enrolled among the saved. As with the story of the Sheep and the Goats, this judgment is based upon what has been done during life (Revelation 20:12). Yet salvation is not pictured as the wages of a good life, but is the free gift of God which is linked to faith in Christ. The final emphasis is not upon salvation by good deeds, but upon the wonder of being enrolled by the Lamb of God in his book of life.

We do not know how God will save those who have never had the opportunity of hearing of Christ's salvation during their life on earth. The New Testament, including Jesus Christ himself, speaks of those who will be lost as well as those who will be saved. It would be reasonable to suppose that those who hear of Jesus Christ, and deliberately refuse him, will be among the lost. But the Bible is silent about those who have never heard, or never heard adequately.

Perhaps the nearest statement is in Romans 2:14-16, where after writing in 1:18-32 of the shocking state of the Gentile world, Paul says, "When Gentiles who do not have the law do by nature what the law requires, they are a law to themselves, even though they do not have the law. They show that what the law requires is written on their hearts, while their conscience also bears witness, and their conflicting thoughts accuse or perhaps excuse them on that day when, according to my gospel, God judges the secrets of men by Christ Jesus."

Paul wrote this, although in the same letter he made the strongest statements about salvation as the free gift of God only through faith in Jesus Christ. Whatever is the way in which God brings to salvation anyone who has never heard of Christ, we can be absolutely certain that there is no salvation except through Christ.

If at the judgment any non-Christian is welcomed into eternal life, he will understand that Christ is his Saviour. No one will be saved except through Christ. This is hinted at in the parable of the Sheep and the Goats; and in the passage in Revelation 20:11-15 the final emphasis is not upon the good works, but upon the name being written in the book of life, which as we have seen is the Lamb's book of life.

None of us dares presume to understand the ways of God in saving mankind. When Jesus was asked, "Lord, will those who are saved be few?" he threw the question back, "Strive to enter by the narrow door." It is as though he said, "Act as though there will be few, and make sure you are among them." But then he partially answered the question, "Many, I tell you, will seek to enter and will not be able," and went on to describe the tragic state of those who are left outside (Luke 13:23-30).

We are glad to believe that God has a door that is open wider than we may have imagined, but again and again we read of many who are lost. Many of us now think of these as having closed the door of heaven against themselves. It would be strange if those who have lived happily without God in this world should actually enjoy the bliss of the presence of God in heaven. This has never been better shown than by CS Lewis in his book *The Great Divorce*.

The nature of hell is a mystery. Some traditional views have seemed so inconsistent with the character of

God that people have rejected the fact of hell altogether, which to my mind is a view that cannot be argued from the Bible.

Other Bible believers, including myself, accept that hell is eternal, but that it is eternal death and destruction, and not everlasting existence in torment. This can be gathered from the Bible, once one is prepared to break from the traditional pattern of interpretation. The terrible sense of loss of identity, as one is blotted out, will indeed be torment.

After writing this sentence, I came across a quotation from a philosopher, Miguel de Unamuno. "Not death, something worse, a sensation of annihilation, a supreme anguish." It is difficult for a Christian to feel this, but if one knew that one would never wake up again after an anaesthetic, then the gradual loss of consciousness would indeed be torment. The preservation of sinners for ever would mean that the universe was never cleaned from sin.

This is not the place to argue about the nature of hell. Whatever form it takes, Christ came to deliver us from it. This was one step in the simple purpose of the incarnation, and the other step was to be Lord of all.

CHAPTER 13
THE PERFECT MAN

In 1955 I wrote a book, *What is Man?* (Paternoster Press), which was later revised as *Mind, Man and the Spirits* and *Man in the Process of Time*. I find that the closing chapter summarises so much of what I have written in this book, and clarifies it, that it is worth reprinting here.

THE PERFECT MAN
There has been only one perfect Man, Jesus Christ. No book on the nature of man could be complete without some consideration of him, however inadequate such consideration must be. The Christian church has always regarded him as both fully God and fully Man, while not professing to understand the mystery of what is technically called *the hypostatic union*.

The Gospel records show that he was truly Man, and no divine apparition ... he entered the world by the gateway of birth, and passed through the normal stages of growth and development (Luke 2:52). His body needed to be sustained by ordinary means. He suffered hunger (Luke 4:2) and thirst (John 19:28) and often felt the strain of weariness (Mark 4:38; John 4:6). Being a man, he experienced the attacks of temptation through various channels (Matthew 4:1-11), though on no occasion did he fall into sin. Finally he died a real death in fearful agony. There is no doubt that he was Man.

Yet in certain ways he appeared to be more than Man. He claimed for himself powers which logically belong to God alone. Thus he claimed to have power to forgive sins (Matthew 9:2-7; Luke 7:48-50) and to be the final Judge of men (Matthew 7:21-23; 13:41-43; 25:31-33; Mark 13:26-27). He drew men to himself in a way that no mere man ought to do, pointing to himself as the giver of eternal life in response to faith in himself (John 6:47-51), as the source of comfort and rest (Matthew 11:28), and as the One without whom no man could come to the Father (John 14:6) or know the Father (Matthew 11:27). He claimed that between his Father and himself there existed a unique union (Matthew 11:27; John 10:28-30). Further, he claimed to have had a pre-existence with his Father (John 6:62; 8:58; 16:28; 17:4-5,24).

Some texts are more precise, though we have not space for all. In John 1:1 he is the Word, and the "Word was God". The Greek does not mean "the Word was divine", as Jehovah's Witnesses assert. In John 20:28 Jesus accepts the worship of Thomas, when he says, "My Lord and my God." In Philippians 2:6 Jesus is said to have been "in the form of God", where Paul uses a word for *form* that means *essential being*. In Hebrews 1:8 he, as the Son, is addressed as God: "But of the Son he says, "Thy throne, O God, is for ever and ever, the righteous sceptre is the sceptre of thy kingdom."

In the book of the Revelation he is on the Throne of God and is worshipped as God (Revelation 5). Moreover, there are the well-known words that are so often used at the conclusion of services, taken from 2 Corinthians 13:14, "The Grace of the Lord Jesus Christ, and the love of God and the fellowship of the Holy Spirit be with you all." The position and order of the Names in the sentence would be blasphemous if Christ were not God.

One problem that has vexed the church is the relation of the Deity to the Manhood during the incarnation. Some have supposed that Christ emptied himself of his Deity during his incarnate life, so that he virtually ceased to be God – in fact he came so far under human limitations as to be subject to human errors on points of fact. This is often called the Kenosis theory, the title being taken from the Greek word in Philippians 2:7 (RV "emptied himself"; KJV "made himself of no reputation").

Yet the New Testament declares that it was while he was upholding all things by the word of his power, that he died for our sins (Hebrews 1:3). The reference here is to the divine sustaining of the universe in being, which is ascribed to Christ as the Second Person of the Trinity. So also it is said in Colossians 1:17, "In him all things hold together." To suppose that Christ could virtually cease to be God, suggests for the Christian the impossible conception that the Trinity could become a Duality, and so God is not essentially a Trinity.

But if Christ was God, with the attributes of Godhead while he was on earth, how can his human existence be saved from artificiality? It cannot be solved by assuming two watertight compartments of his being, so that for example he did his miracles as God, and ate and slept as Man. Such ideas tend to resolve Christ into two separate persons.

It is probable that the view of man's nature taken here has some light to throw on the problem, though I think that only two theologians have attempted this approach. They are W Sandy in *Christologies, Ancient and Modern* (OUP, 1910), and *Personality in Christ and in Ourselves* (Clarendon, 1911); and WR Matthews in *The Problem of Christ in the Twentieth Century* (OUP, 1950), though in what follows I am not entirely reproducing their views.

The mind of an ordinary man has the two main divisions of conscious and unconscious. The unconscious is the storehouse of memories, and the place of the dynamic urges of life. The unconscious is, as its name suggests, necessarily unknown directly by the conscious mind, but from it come memories and forces that influence the conscious. Fallen men and women have but a poor control of the gateway between conscious and unconscious. Memories and thoughts flash through the gate when they are not wanted, and fail to appear when they are summoned.

But one imagines that a perfect man would have perfect control of the gate. Only those things would flow into consciousness which he desired to admit. Now Jesus Christ was a perfect Man. His divine knowledge and powers were below the threshold of consciousness, and would not flow into his consciousness unless he chose to allow them to do so.

While he was on earth he chose to draw only upon human capacities for his daily living. Many of his miracles may have been done because he was perfect Man. Some may have come through the inflowing of his Deity. In his human spirit he held unbroken communion with his Father; he gave the teachings which his Father gave him to speak (for example John 8:47; 14:10,24).

There were certain things which he was not commissioned to teach, and consequently he did not allow them to flow into his human consciousness. Such was the date of his Second Coming, of which he declares that he, as the incarnate Son, is ignorant (Mark 13:32).

Because he was Man, his brain and mind needed to grow and develop (Luke 2:52). Human knowledge, which comes piece by piece, is of a different order from divine simultaneous knowledge. One might take as an illustration the knowledge of an architect who knows the house before a brick is laid, and the knowledge of a labourer who comes to know the house as he lays brick on brick. In the incarnation, the Architect became the

Builder.

The divine function which Colossians 1:17 and Hebrews 1:3 ascribe to Christ, is that of sustaining the Universe in being. We have spoken of the life-principle flowing through the world, the energy of the creative God, and have seen that this emerges in every man to maintain him in life. May we then be bold enough to hold that, in the incarnate Lord, this impersonal energy did not flow in alone but flowed out as well? This energy does not form part of the consciousness of men; nor need it have formed part of the consciousness of Christ. The creative and sustaining work of the universe continued because Christ was still linked to the universe.

Another fact may emerge from the incarnation. We have become aware of a contact of mind with mind at a deep level. There may be something akin to the Collective Unconscious of Jung, linking the human race together. If scientific discovery compelled us to suppose that there were other beings of human status at the time when Adam was created (and I do not think it does), we could still postulate that the whole human race was put "in Adam" by being linked, mind with mind, at a deep level, and that the fall of Adam dragged all others down with him. But at least it is likely that, if there is a group mind of humanity in any sense of the word, it is disordered by sin.

By becoming Man, Jesus Christ became linked to this corporate mind of man, or at least telepathically involved with every other man, though he is like the current of fresh water in an ocean of salt. Now we have seen that at this level, mind overrides the normal sequence of time and is in some way linked with what we call past, present and future.

How did Christ on the cross, two thousand years ago, bear the sins that I have committed today? Could it be that he drew me there in the depths of my personality, with all my sins, and made my sinful personality his own? When Christ died, all humanity died, because he, the second Adam, had involved himself in the human race, past, present and future.

Dare we go further? This One who died *was* the sustainer of the universe: he was one with it as its source of life. Obviously his Deity did not cease to exist when he died on the cross, any more than his *Nephesh** ceased to exist. But this suffering on the cross involved that Creative Energy that sustained the universe, and the agony of his Being was reflected in the strangely darkened sun – the light of the world – and in the earthquake.

The centre of the life of the universe suffered human death in that supreme act of atonement and reconciliation, so that Paul can view the atonement as cosmic in its scope. "Through him to reconcile to himself all things, whether on earth or in heaven, making peace by the blood of his cross" (Colossians 1:20). And again, Paul pictures the whole creation as being delivered,

---

* Publisher's footnote: *Nephesh* (נֶפֶשׁ) is an OT Hebrew word which is usually translated as *soul, self,* or *life*.

when the sons of God are manifested in their final state of redemption (Romans 8:18-25).

What does this mean? We dare not say. It is something beyond imagination. We must, I am certain, stop short of universalism. Everything must be delivered according to its own order of being. New heavens and new earth can arise, transformed from the ruins of the old that are shot through with sin. But men and women are beings who must be saved by deliberate response to God: they are free beings, who may repudiate their place in the redemption of the cross. But those who come to Christ in repentance and trust, come to meet One whom they have met before. They met him before they had an existence at all. They were there when he was crucified.

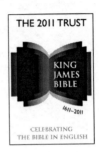

MARY JONES
AND HER BIBLE
AN ADVENTURE BOOK

Mary Jones saved for six years to buy a Bible of her own. In 1800, when she was 15, she thought she had saved enough, so she walked barefoot for 26 miles (more than 40km) over a mountain pass and through deep valleys in Wales to get one. That's when she discovered there were none for sale!

You can travel with Mary Jones today in this book by following clues, or just reading the story. Either way, you will get to Bala where Mary went, and if you're really quick you may be able to discover a Bible just like Mary's in the market!

The true story of Mary Jones has captured the imagination for more than 200 years. For this book, Chris Wright has looked into the old records and discovered even more of the story, which is now in this unforgettable account of Mary Jones and her Bible. Solving puzzles is part of the fun, but the whole story is in here to read and enjoy whether you try the puzzles or not. Just turn the page, and the adventure continues. It's time to get on the trail of Mary Jones!

A true story with optional puzzles.
(Some are easy, some tricky, and some amusing.)
Published by Christian publishers White Tree Publishing
ISBN 978-0-9525956-2-5
5.5 x 8.5 inches paperback
UK £6.95, €8.95, US $12.95
156 pages of story, photographs, line drawings and puzzles.
The full story of Mary Jones's and her Bible
with a clear Christian message.

Lightning Source UK Ltd.
Milton Keynes UK
UKOW020221191011

180542UK00001B/17/P